DEMOCRACY AND THE NEWS

DEMOCRACY
and the NEWS

HERBERT J. GANS

OXFORD
UNIVERSITY PRESS

2003

OXFORD
UNIVERSITY PRESS

Oxford   New York
Auckland   Bangkok   Buenos Aires
Cape Town   Chennai   Dar es Salaam   Delhi   Hong Kong   Istanbul
Karachi   Kolkata   Kuala Lumpur   Madrid   Melbourne   Mexico City   Mumbai
Nairobi   São Paulo   Shanghai   Taipei   Tokyo   Toronto

Published by Oxford University Press, Inc.
198 Madison Avenue, New York, New York 10016

www.oup.com

Oxford is a registered trademark of Oxford University Press

Library of Congress Cataloging-in-Publication Data
Gans, Herbert J.
Democracy and the news / by Herbert J. Gans.
p. cm.
Includes index.
ISBN 0-19-515132-1
1.   Journalism—Political aspects—United States.
2.   Journalism—United States.
I. Title.
PN4888.PG G36 2003

302.23'45'0973   dc21   2002006689

1 3 5 7 9 10 8 6 4 2

Printed in the United States of America
on acid-free paper

For Louise and David

CONTENTS

PREFACE

When I was a young man, I wanted to become a journalist, for I imagined journalism to be the best way to learn about American society. I discovered later that I was more comfortable with sociological research and writing, but I have never lost my admiration for journalists and their work.

My feelings about American democracy also go back a long time, natural perhaps because I arrived in the United States as a refugee from Nazi Germany, where democracy had been terminated. I have written about both journalism and democracy before, but this book links the subjects between the covers of one volume.

Actually, the book is about an ideal democracy, the political part of the American Dream: the country really belongs to the citizenry and its elected representatives, from the president on down; they are ultimately only there to do our bidding. I call this ideal citizens' democracy. Journalists also embrace this ideal, and consider it their work to inform people so that they can carry out their democratic responsibilities.

In this book, I take the ideal seriously, but also use it to look at the reality, actual representative democracy. In addition, I write about the roles that journalists and the news media play in it. Alternating between an ideal and reality, I ask what the news media and journalists are and are not doing to help democracy. I ask further what else journalists could do, and what other, primarily political measures are needed to make American democracy more representative of and for the citizenry.

Sad to say, the news alone cannot contribute as much to democracy as journalists would like. Despite much disingenuous talk about citizen empowerment by politicians and merchandisers, citizens have never had much clout. Countries as big as America operate largely through organizations, including corporations, public agencies, and nonprofits, that can virtually function without citizens, and that citizens have a hard time challenging.

Journalists (a term I use broadly for people who work as newspaper and magazine reporters, writers, editors, and their radio, television, and now internet, equivalents) also have less power than is attributed to them. Most people do not need the news to live their lives, using it to keep up with the world except when world-shaking events such as 9/11 take place.

In effect, many citizens do not much want to be informed, in part because they lack trust in their government's and country's leaders to respond to their concerns. They also mistrust the news media, in part because journalists devote much of the news to the exploits and pronouncements of the leaders in which people lack trust.

I am sometimes critical of journalists and today's journalism, but first and foremost, my analysis targets these structures, the news media, news firms, and movers and shakers to which they are beholden. I write mostly about national journalists and news media in general, largely ignoring differences between print and electronic news media. I also suggest changes in the news that might help make American democracy more responsive to the citizenry. But the truly necessary changes are political and economic. For example, in a society in which giant organizations are influential, citizens may need giant organizations of their own, and in a country in which economic power spells political power, economic democracy must be discussed alongside political democracy.

The Organization of the Book

This book is an extended essay, and its structure resembles that of an onion. The first and last chapters focus primarily on the country, whereas the four inner chapters deal with the news media and the journalists. Chapter 1 examines the place of citizens in the American economy and polity. Chapter 2 analyzes the journalists' place. Chapter 3 lays out some of the problems raised by journalism's mass production and other traditional practices. Chapter 4 offers observations about the effects of the news on individuals and institutions. Chapter 5 presents my ideas for change in the news media and the final chapter, those for moving the country towards a citizens' democracy some day and a more representative one now.

ACKNOWLEDGMENTS

My first thanks go to Everette Dennis, the founder of the Media Studies Center, and to Jerry Sass, whose idea it was in the first place. Everette Dennis nominated me for a Center Fellowship in 1996; his successors enabled me to use that year to start thinking about this book. (I am sorry that the Freedom Forum organization has now eliminated both the fellowship program and the center itself.)

While at the center, I received help and support from my fellow fellows and more staff members than I can name. Consequently, I will mention only Arlene Morgan from among the fellows, and Larry McGill from its staff. My thanks also to Dr. Patricia D'Andrade and Jocelyn Boryczka, who put in a semester each as my research assistants at the center.

My Columbia University colleague Robert Shapiro often knew where to find the data I needed, and Darren Chilton first showed me how to find and download other data from the internet. Much of the poll data on which I relied came from the Pew Research Center for the People & the Press, and I am grateful to its director, Andrew Kohut, for his help. Several other research centers that extended help are mentioned in the endnotes.

I am also indebted to a number of people who helped me over the years. Among fellow sociologists, the principal ones were Michael Schudson and Todd Gitlin; among journalists, Reuven Frank and the late Edwin Diamond. Information and ideas also came from the many journalists whom I read and to whom I listened about the problems of their profession. I learned yet more from the countless number with whom I spoke at meetings, conferences, seminars, and lectures on journalism and the news media during the years I worked on this book. The mistakes in the book are all mine.

ACKNOWLEDGMENTS

I am particularly grateful to my editor, Tim Bartlett. He line edited the manuscript above and beyond the call of duty, looking out for the general reader while I was focused on journalist, social scientist, and student readers. I also thank his assistant, Farahnaz Maroof, as well as Paula Cooper for her empathetic copyediting and Catherine Humphries for her dedicated production editing.

Herbert J. Gans
June 2002

DEMOCRACY AND THE NEWS

CHAPTER 1

Citizens' Democracy and
Citizen Disempowerment

According to the American Dream, American democracy belongs to its citizens and America might therefore be called a "citizens' democracy." The country is formally considered a representative democracy, but the representatives are supposed to be guided by the citizenry, through voting and participating in other ways. Elected officials from the president on down may ultimately make the decisions, but they are still seen as doing the citizens' bidding: acting as surrogates for them between elections. Although elected representatives stand in for the citizenry, they too are supposed to "belong" to the citizens.

Journalists also follow the Dream, but they add an informational provision. The country's democracy may belong directly or indirectly to its citizens, but the democratic process can only be truly meaningful if these citizens are informed. Journalism's job is to inform them.[1] As *New York Times* columnist Anthony Lewis ended his last column before retirement, "The most important office in a democracy, Justice Louis Brandeis said, is the office of citizen."[2] In an earlier column, he defined the journalist's role: "The theory of democracy is that the citizens are the ultimate sovereign. But in today's world, individuals cannot personally observe events and reach decisions in a forum, as in ancient Athens. They necessarily depend on the press to be informed."[3] Or, as author and news executive Jack Fuller writes: "The central purpose of journalism is to tell the truth so that people will have the information that they need to be sovereign."[4]

The Dream is an ideal. Most everyone would like to believe it, including the journalists, even as they are kept busy reporting the functioning and malfunctioning of America's real democracy. The ideal democracy lacks a society, an economy, class, power, and other structures, and there is no mention of firms, agencies, and other organizations. Indeed, in the ideal democracy that underlies the Dream, elected representatives are absent, even though the democracy itself does not appear to be a direct one. Not surprisingly, the ideal democracy has ideal citizens: a single and often single-minded public that leaves out the real citizens with opposing interests, beliefs, and values.[5] In this and other respects, the Dream is much too simplistic.

The Dream's value lies in its goal: to establish a viable democratic role for the citizenry. Its value also lies in the central question it raises: what should and can that role be in a country as vast as the United States? What can citizens do if such a country is dominated by organizations big enough to discourage citizens from challenging them, and powerful enough to usually defeat those who try to do so? What can the public do if their elected representatives have had to rent or sell pieces of themselves to such organizations in order to be elected?

I do not propose that citizens are good and organizations evil, or that a greater role for citizens would necessarily lead to a better country. However, if one essential goal of democracy is to represent the interests of all the people, as much as that is possible in a heterogeneous nation, then more effective means of representation must be developed.

The Power of Organizations

The central political role of the citizenry is usually taken so much for granted that it is not often discussed. In fact, that role is thought to be taken care of by the elections. The news media continue to reinforce the idea, particularly through their continuous and detailed coverage of election campaign events (and nonevents), almost as if the never-ending coverage could prove that the citizenry still holds the ultimate power. In some respects, this is even true, because when the winning candidates are willing, able, or required to make good on some of their campaign promises, then the citizenry may indeed have played a powerful role.

The citizens themselves are also realistic, however, for every year that poll respondents are asked, an increasing number, ever closer to a majority, thinks that who they elect president makes no significant political difference. Business journalist John Quirt once put that belief graphically, describing "Washington as a brothel where the privileged princes of perk and pork enjoy themselves while ordinary folks elect a new piano player every four years."[6] Economist James K. Galbraith made the same point more politely: describing America as a corporate democracy, he sees the voters as "shareholders, owners in title only . . . [casting] their votes in periodic referenda."[7]

In addition, poll respondents believe the country is run by Big Government, Big Business—and surprisingly enough also by Big Unions, even if few of these still have a sizable amount of power.[8] The conclusion, like the poll question that generated it, is too simple, and some or even much of the time, Big Government acts as it does because it is being pressed to do so by Big Business and to a lesser extent by once Big Unions and others.[9]

More important, the old trinity has become a quartet, the newest member being Big NGOs: nongovernmental organizations such as professional and trade associations, lobbies, foundations, and the array of major political, cultural, educational, religious, environmental, and other nonprofit organizations. Between 1980 and 1997, the number of nonprofit organizations increased from nearly 15,000 to nearly 23,000.[10]

Despite their diverse and often opposing goals and interests, these organizations, be they businesses, unions, or NGOs share at least one characteristic: they are formally organized, bureaucratized with a limited number of objectives that they pursue as single-mindedly and rationally as they can. They are not necessarily partisan but they are nevertheless directly and indirectly political organizations. However nonpolitical their mission statements, they seek and use political influence to achieve their objectives, to grow in influence and size, control their markets or turfs when possible, and make alliances with each other if relevant. I think of them as formal organizations to contrast them with the informal groups: families, friends, neighbors, and fellow workers in which citizens spend most of their lives.

Many of the big organizations are getting bigger, and as two or more merge, others must also, to keep pace. In addition, big organizations find it easiest to work with other big organizations, creating yet another impetus for mergers. Even some of the nonprofits among them command massive resources, hire cheap labor, and engineer mergers. Universities shift more teaching positions to poorly paid adjunct professors and graduate students, although unlike hospitals, they have not yet begun to merge. Nonprofits and NGOs do not make profits, but they operate in many respects like private firms, and their executives associate with, or are recruited from among, their corporate peers.

Citizens seem to be resigned to their lack of power in the world of organizations, and in reality may not even want power, often seeking instead to maximize control over the parts of their lives that matter to them. They buy goods and services from the big corporations, and obtain relevant aid and support from the government, but they cannot possibly compete with the single-mindedness—or the skillful hired hands—of formal organizations. In fact, most citizens often cannot even see, or do not care to see what these organizations and the public officials they elect do below the radar at which individual citizens live their lives.

In any big country that fondly remembers its humble beginnings, small is usually preferable to big, informal is superior to formal, and the citizenry is better than the formal organizations. However this Manichean view can be excessive. In a vast society, many organizations are apt to be big and as the society expands so do its organizations. Moreover, as the world becomes interdependent, organizations become multinational, and therefore yet bigger. Big is not intrinsically evil, however, and big organizations can be beneficial to the citizenry. What distinguishes these organizations from citizens are the economic and political powers they bring to the democratic table. At issue is the unequal balance of power between them rather than merely size, because that inequality per se will likely hurt the citizenry. What matters, therefore, is whether it can be reduced or controlled sufficiently to preserve a viable democratic role for the citizenry.

The balance between citizens and organizations may have been less unequal in the old days but otherwise, the past was hardly superior to the present. Powerful organizations have been around for a long time in one form or another. Current analyses worry mostly about conglomerates and multinationals.[11] In earlier years, interlocking directorates, trusts, unions, and "bureaucracy" were viewed as the major threats. Historically, the culprits included large family firms and individual entrepreneurs (read: robber barons), kings, nobles, and the economic agencies and agents they controlled. This kind of analysis can probably be traced back at least to the time that hunter-gatherers became sedentary and began to acquire unequal amounts of property and power. Whatever the character of these organizations, unorganized citizens have almost always lost out.

The first time he visited America, Alexis de Tocqueville expressed a great deal of interest in informal, social, and other voluntary associations and the popular joining thereof, but were he to come back today, he might ask himself why he did not pay more attention to the economic and other formal organizations of the 1830s. While he would still call attention to the country's individualism, he might also note that the personal freedoms of the citizenry are more limited than he once thought.

Despite the endless parade of politicians who promise more empowerment to their constituents, we live in a country in which the normal state of the citizenry is "disempowerment." The term is clumsy but it is also graphic. In addition, the term suggests that a process is taking place, which in turn raises the question of whether the influence of unorganized citizens, or even organized ones, is changing—or declining.

Economic Disempowerment

American citizens are experiencing both economic and political disempowerment. Mergers and takeovers are perhaps the most potent catalysts of citizen disempowerment because many are followed by the elimination of jobs, and the concurrent increase of inequality among those who must take jobs that pay less and offer less security. Additionally, when American firms ship their operations overseas, their accountability, other than to shareholders, moves with them as well. During periods of economic expansion, jobs are regained, although in the United States as elsewhere, income and wealth inequality have not declined during the most recent growth periods. When management presses for higher profits, either because of fears of a takeover, or shareholder demands, more people lose their jobs, whether the times are good or bad. When executives cook the books or otherwise bankrupt their firms, the workers are likely to lose their retirement monies as well.

The country's economic centralization is masked in part by the continuing growth spurts of small businesses. Most new businesses are small ones, and countrywide the average number of employees per business is still only about 20. Presumably that growth will continue as long as new inventions lead to new industries that start as small businesses, except that in the longer run, the big fish eat many of the small fish, then merge with each other. The number of mergers and acquisitions increased from 1,719 in 1985 to 9,634 in 1999.[12]

Small businesses usually pay less than large ones, and so do businesses that provide "services"—except when the services are rendered by professionals. Much of the economic boom of the late 1990s was fueled by a growth in minimum- and other low-wage employment, and there is no reason to believe that this pattern will change. The manufacturing jobs, particularly unionized ones, that provided secure jobs and incomes have declined considerably. Although computerization has created new jobs, many of these also pay low wages, even if the exotically technical high-wage positions have obtained much of the publicity. Still, the lowest wages are paid to welfare recipients who have been put to work to earn their benefits, for which they are in effect receiving subminimum wages. Nonetheless, the economic powerlessness of low-wage workers and the social and emotional powerlessness that accompanies it is undoubtedly felt most intensely by people who have been downsized from well-paying jobs, for example, the autoworkers who have become security guards and the secretaries who had to turn to waitressing.[13]

Another form of economic disempowerment follows from the shedding of employer obligations. These include the reduction or elimination of employee benefits, notably pensions and health insurance, and the shift to several kinds of contingent employment, although so far only among a small, if slowly rising proportion, of the labor force.

Even when they are well paid, workers who are hired as involuntary part-timers, temps, and independent (but still involuntary) contractors lose the economic power that accompanies job security. So far, only a small proportion of the labor force is in contingent jobs, and some people prefer such jobs, but the number of people who will spend their work lives in contingent work of one kind or another is likely to increase. Firms undergoing downturns or unusual competition shift to contingent work to maximize their flexibility, but many then find that such flexibility pays off in additional profits even when good times return.

The most drastic economic disempowerment is reserved for those who are pushed out of the job market or have never entered it. The prototypical example are those among the immense number of incarcerated young people who are in prison for petty drug selling, itself an illegal form of low-wage employment, and other minor nonviolent or victimless crimes. Prison constitutes total economic disempowerment, which becomes permanent if ex-felons do not find jobs.

The new employment arrangements that spell lower incomes and less security can be viewed as a comprehensive power shift that cuts across the entire economy. In this shift, power has moved further from unionized and other blue- and white-collar workers to technicians and professionals, but even more power has shifted to major stockholders in and executives and owners of medium and larger businesses.

Most economic power shifts alter the distribution of income and wealth. The result, in America as well as elsewhere, has been a drastic rise in economic inequality since the 1970s. For example, between 1979 and 1997, the incomes of families in the middle of the income distribution rose 9 percent, while the incomes of families in the top 1 percent rose 140 percent, from $420,000 per year to over one million.[14]

However, inequality is not merely a loss of economic power. It has social and emotional repercussions as well. Researchers are now discovering that when people are downwardly mobile and become economically and socially more unequal, they also suffer from declining health, more family breakups, and increased social isolation. In particular, the process of downward mobility often produces lower self-esteem and lack of self-confidence that bring on depression and interfere with the ability to respond to opportunity. Inequality thus has negative effects of its own, above and beyond those stemming from low income and status.[15]

In addition, economic inequality has political effects, because the less than equal tend to vote less often, are politically less visible in other ways, and thus are not likely to attract politicians eager to represent them. The poor also lose from the decline and gradual elimination of the welfare state, including now-eliminated, emasculated, or privatized programs in community medicine and public health, job creation, occupational safety, and the like.

Despite the continuing disempowerment of the citizenry, we should resist the temptation to demonize corporations and other large organizations. A large society will probably always be dominated by large organizations. If citizens are to obtain more power or representation, the rules that govern such organizations must be altered, particularly those governing their freedom to use their economic strengths to enhance their political power.

The various kinds of economic and related disempowerment described above may even turn out to be temporary, although that seems unlikely. The economic boom of the mid- and late-1990s and the subsequent economic downturn testify to the continued existence of the traditional business cycle. Private enterprise remains risky, as illustrated by the rapid rise and fall of so many dot coms, hence the willingness and ability of firms to take risks must be protected. Still, placing many of the costs of these risks on workers and other citizens is not justified. Why should workers be laid off more often than dividends, and why should citizen taxpayers have to cushion the risks taken by firms as often as they are required to do?

Today's business cycles may also be diverging from old ones. Over time, the use of cyclical ups and downs to eliminate jobs (especially among merged firms exploiting the economy of scale), the resort to computers and other new technologies to shift economic activity further away from labor-intensive and more toward capital-intensive activities, and the shipping of jobs overseas could produce further economic disempowerment. Professional and other highly skilled workers may always be needed, but well-paying and reasonably secure jobs seem to be most vulnerable. The late 1990s demonstrated that the U.S. economy can boom while employing contingent and minimum wage workers, even welfare recipients earning subminimum wages on workfare. It can also shed workers during downward turns of the business cycle but not rehire as many of them when good times return, thus increasing the vulnerability of these workers.

The end of the boom may demonstrate another new (or forgotten old) economic fact of life: computers, robots, robotic machines, and foreign workers can replace American workers, but firms selling consumer goods, as well as all the manufacturing, processing, and other firms selling to them cannot survive without American customers. Consumers have one economic weapon that is hard to eliminate and could become increasingly significant for the country's economic health: they are needed to buy what the economy produces. Recall that not so long after the 9/11 tragedy, President Bush and New York Mayor Rudolph Giuliani urged Americans to resume buying as quickly as possible.

Bush and Giuliani's appeal should also remind us what they, like other Republicans, often wish to forget: economic institutions do not exist apart from political ones, and the economic disempowerment of citizens goes hand in hand with political disempowerment.

Political Disempowerment

The interplay of economic and political disempowerment can be traced back at least as far as the invention of Athenian democracy. Even then, slaves lacked a political voice. American independence from England was sought in part for economic reasons, and the Constitution as well as other early legislation generally included provisions beneficial to the economically powerful of the time, including landowners and slaveholders. Since then, the history of American politics has been marked by elected officials voting the interests of major industries or other large employers in their states or districts.

Organizations that benefit or need special treatment from government have traditionally done so by demonstrating their power, for example, the power to create or move jobs, or taxable incomes that can determine the fates of elected officials. At least one senator from Washington state has usually been known as the Senator from Boeing as long as that company has played an economically influential role in the state. More often, organizations flex their political muscles by hiring lobbyists and by contributing to election campaigns.

In 1999, nearly 4,000 lobbying organizations employing almost 12,000 individual lobbyists were located in Washington, spending nearly 1.5 billion dollars for lobbying activities.[16]

The number of lobbyists continues to increase slowly but surely, as does the variety of their activities, which affects the already limited power of citizens.[17] Most lobbyists still represent corporate clients, although some also work for trade associations, professional groups, unions, NGOs, and nonprofits. Even universities need lobbyists these days. Lobbies representing people as citizens exist as well, but only on behalf of a still quite limited number of causes.

Big spenders among the lobbyists seem to be determined less by corporate size or power than by the legislative issues in Washington and those raised by electoral candidates who need campaign funds. For example, a 1997 study of major lobbyists reported that the most free-spending industries that year were pharmaceuticals and health products, insurance, and utilities.[18] As might be expected, organizations vary in the proportion of expenditures devoted to lobbying and campaign contributions. In 1997, pharmaceutical and other health products firms spent the most on lobbyists, while investment, real estate, and law firms spent far more on campaign support.[19]

By comparison, citizen groups have little to spend. In 1997, only five of the top 100 spenders could be described as citizen groups, headed by the Christian Coalition and the National Committee to Preserve Social Security. That number rises to eight with the inclusion of the Commonwealth of Puerto Rico, which lobbies hard to bring jobs to the island, and two unions, the AFL-CIO and the United Auto Workers. These are, properly speaking, economic rather than citizen groups, but their spending was so meager that they ranked only seventy-sixth and ninety-sixth respectively among the top hundred.[20] In fact, unions obtain most of their political strength by their ability to bring a proportion of their members to the polls and more important, to persuade them to campaign for candidates being supported by the union.

Most of the other citizen groups were additional organizations representing seniors, including the American Association of Retired Persons (AARP). The kinds of people and causes that citizen organizations represent remains tiny. The only good news for citizens is that citizen lobbies have grown in number in the last half century, increasing from 15 to 24 percent of lobbies between 1960 and 1995.[21]

Nonetheless, the limited power of citizens is restricted still further because even their big organizations lack the single-mindedness of their opposition. Perhaps the best example is the AARP, for while it has over 30 million mostly middle-aged and older members, they come from all points in the political and ideological spectrum and thus disagree on many policies. As a result, the AARP could not take a strong stand in support of the Clinton and other health policy reform proposals, while hospital, private health insurance, and other associations used their greater unity of purpose, as well of course as their lobbies, campaign aid, and various kinds of economic power, to beat back reforms. A hospital executive who as a private citizen supports Republicans is unlikely to act differently on behalf of his or her institution than one who votes for Democrats.

In addition, lobbies, like other political organizations function at times as if they were citizens' groups. Some regularly create outpourings of engineered public opinion that can impress legislators and that are sometimes crucial in passing legislation when the vote is close. Admittedly, the engineered opinions probably reflect the feelings of the people who send e-mails, letters, and wires, but few are spontaneous, and opposing views are marginalized in the process. Citizen groups also organize letter-writing campaigns, that at least represent citizens' opinions. Still, polls, that obtain opinions from a sample of the entire population are far more democratic.

Most of the time, lobbyists do not need to resort to such activities, because they operate mainly through that mysterious process called "access," both for themselves and for their clients. Many lobbyists are former elected officials themselves, and are thus trusted, which may also help them keep their opponents, including ordinary citizens and their lobbies, from obtaining access.

Though access can be politely pro forma, the correlation between what lobbyists request and what elected officials will give is high enough to make lobbying worthwhile and influential. Much of what is given may be in the public interest, but corporations can obtain the legislation, contracts, and government subsidies that increase profits but may raise prices for citizens. I use the word "correlation" deliberately, as correlations are not causes, and most of the time, proof that a public official's decision was caused by the lobbyists' access to that official is hard to come by. Also, it is always possible that an elected official can vote his or her conscience and simultaneously accept a campaign donation from an organization benefitting from that vote.

Journalists regularly report the correlations but evidently people either do not notice, are resigned to them, or may not care because the financial and other costs to them of each successful lobbying effort are inconsequential. However, the lobbyists and the lobbied also try to keep their activities below the political radar at which beltway doings are visible.[22]

Lobbying works effectively for all but the most popular issues, but it works even better when the lobbyists or their clients also help supply campaign funds.[23] Even when elections are not close, every campaign always seems to be able to use more money. The largest share of the money is spent to pay for television advertising to reach voters and potential voters, and most of that money goes to station owners who are able to charge high prices for television time.

One explanation for the continuing rise in campaign expenditures and television advertising is that potential voters are becoming harder to reach, and that more money must be spent to persuade them not only to vote but to vote for the candidate and party doing the advertising. No one has tested the accuracy of this explanation or studied to what extent people's unwillingness to be reached reflected their satisfaction with the status quo, their unhappiness with elections, or with politics in general.

Whether the increase in campaign spending can ever be stopped remains to be seen. Although Congress banned the use of "soft" money in 2002 for this purpose, the courts still have to rule on the constitutionality of the ban. In addition, the Supreme Court has to overturn or temper its decision that campaign money is equivalent to "speech" and thus protected by the Bill of Rights. Moreover, the 2002 legislation has enough loopholes to enable campaign funders to keep the money flowing, even if they may have to ship it to different receiving agencies than before.

Voters are disempowered in other ways by the high costs of running for office. Not only do election winners often have to take care of their major contributors ahead of their constituents, but they may have less time to represent their constituents because of the time they must spend raising campaign money.

The financial pressure is such that a growing number of Congressional incumbents do not stand for reelection because they dislike the endless fundraising or are no good at it. In the future, the same pressure could also attract more candidates who are especially able and willing to fund raise, like to associate with campaign funders, and are more comfortable with them than with their rank-and-file constituents.

Another set of victims of costlier elections may be liberal candidates and those representing racial minorities, especially if they run on issues opposed by free-spending corporations. Conservatives argue that liberals can always count on union help to get out the vote, but many unions are no longer as liberal or as strong as in the past. Moreover, liberals cannot obtain the equivalent of the conservatives' foundation-funded issues research as well as the publications and press conferences that promote and spread the messages of conservative candidates at no cost to them.[24]

The most serious victims are, as always, poor and moderate-income people. They are already disempowered more than other citizens, but lose further power because candidates who speak to their needs and demands cannot afford to campaign, and some may not even want to run. Candidates who speak for the poor may be denounced by others as "demagogues," and may find it more politically advantageous for their political futures to represent wealthier folks. As a result, even fewer poor people can be persuaded to vote, which then further discourages potential candidates who would like to represent them.

The result is a disempowerment spiral. Moreover, thanks to current campaign practices and voting patterns, the same spiral could grow far beyond the poor, advantaging prosperous voters at the political expense of the less affluent, despite the fact that they outnumber them. The spiral may in fact have begun, for the proportion of "upscale" voters in the total electorate has increased while there has been a sizeable and continuing decline of voting by moderate-income and poor voters for more than a half century.[25] Media researcher Robert McChesney has estimated that the richest fifth of the population now supplies half the votes in presidential elections.[26] The systematic discouragement of black voters and sabotage of black votes that helped George Bush obtain the official Florida voting margin he needed to win the 2000 election, and that surely takes place in many other states, adds further to the spiral. Admittedly, the spiral halts when issues or candidates popular with a large enough number of less properous voters return to the voting booth, but the continuously low turnout in national elections—half of registered voters during presidential election years and about a third when only congressional candidates are up for election—suggests that the spiral remains alive and well.

Most worrying, however, is the possibility that an informal alliance of big organizations, campaign funders, and upscale voters who agree with their politics could form and encourage elected officials as well as candidates to pay primary attention to issues and policies favored by member of this alliance. If lower socioeconomic groups, seeing that their needs and demands are less frequently considered by incumbents and challengers, vote even less frequently, they could help turn America into a not-very-democratic upscale democracy.

The Limits of Disempowerment

Organizations and unorganized citizens often have different or conflicting purposes: organizations fight with each other and citizens may themselves be split into various camps. In the abstract, organizations are virtually always more powerful and decisive than citizens, but in practice, organizations and citizens are not locked in permanent or constant conflict. Actually, few conflicts are so dichotomized, as more often different combinations of organizations with groups of citizens on their side, or citizens supported by organizations, are battling another combination of organizations and citizens.

In addition, organizational power is fluid. Even giants can sometimes lose resources, supporters, clients, or functions. Economic power is more solid than political power. Big corporations can suffer severely in the marketplace but they rarely suffer permanent damage. Even movie studios, dressmakers, and others selling goods or services ruled by fashion can usually pick up the pieces after they have backed the wrong horse. Political power is more fragile, because ultimately, enough of the citizenry can agree and then make its numbers felt, at least temporarily.

The numbers do not even need to be all that large, for sometimes political schemes can be derailed by fewer citizens than might be expected in a large society. Not many citizens were needed in 2001 to persuade the White House to restore federal standards for the amount of arsenic in drinking water that President Bush had reduced just after his election.

Sometimes, actual citizens are not even needed; a change in the political "climate" seems to be sufficient. A small rise in the number of letters, e-mails, and phone calls to political leaders, unexpected answers to pollster questions, an apparent consensus on cable television and radio talk shows, and more than the normal quota of editorials in major newspapers can be interpreted as signs of a transformed political climate. In 1998, a change in that climate helped persuade Newt Gingrich to resign from the House of Representatives.

Of course, poll results themselves play important political roles at times, such as before election campaigns are designed when issues are being chosen, and after elections, before policy decisions are made. Moreover, the president's ability to pursue his administration's objectives is influenced by his approval rating, that is, the number of people who say they approve of the way the named incumbent is handling his job as president. People are also asked whether they approve of his performance in various policy areas, for example terrorism or the economy. Although they are not asked about the specifics, the answers to the general approval questions seem to be a politically reliable enough indicator to persuade presidents with a high approval rating that they can pursue their objectives. Because the question is asked constantly, a sudden decline is apt to bring about a change in presidential strategy.

Do People Feel Disempowered?

Although economic and political disempowerment is a fact of American life, whether citizens feel disempowered or not is another question. Actually, they have not even been asked. Politicians have not thought of such a question, and pundits as well as researchers who keep their fingers on the political pulse of the nation do not often discuss it either.

Pollsters, who are for better and worse, the major collectors of the public's thoughts and opinions are mainly interested in what their respondents think about the holders of power, not whether they have any power themselves.[27] Moreover, although the pollsters ask people whether they approve of the president's performance, their questions about other elected, and appointed leaders take a very different tack: whether people "trust" or have "confidence" in these leaders.

As far as I can tell, no one has ever asked the respondents what they think the pollsters mean by trust or confidence, or what they themselves think about these words when they answer the question. Nonetheless, their answers are often given great weight by pundits and others assessing the nation's cohesion or stability.

Strictly speaking, pollsters are actually not surveying what people think, but whether they agree or disagree with statements the pollsters present to them. This technique adds yet another complication to interpreting trust, confidence, and other polling questions, and in what follows I have tried hard to use only polling questions that minimize these problems, and may shed a little light on both economic and political disempowerment.[28]

Economic Disempowerment

Pollsters do not study the citizenry's economic power, but they occasionally ask their respondents about the power of business. Then, many Americans become surprisingly egalitarian. A study by the Pew Research Center for the People & the Press (Pew Center hereafter) reported that during the 1990s, close to 75 percent of the respondents assented to the statement "there is too much power concentrated in the hands of a few big companies." Nearly as many also agreed, and have agreed over the years, that "business corporations make too much profit;"[29] that "the rich get richer and the poor get poorer;"[30] and that both the rich and business pay too few taxes.

Respondents are also asked whether they have confidence in business and its leaders. In 1966, when this question was first asked, over half of those polled had a great deal of confidence in Big Business or major companies. That confidence fell to as low as about 10 percent in bad economic times during the next decades, however, and came back up to only 20 percent in 1998 when the impeachment crisis was ending and the country's economic health was improving.[31]

Political Disempowerment

Confidence in government historically has been slightly lower than confidence in business, and confidence in government leaders is yet slightly lower. Thus, confidence in Congress was 42 percent in 1973 but had declined to 22 percent in 1997.[32] Political scientists S. M. Lipset and William Schneider, who have conducted the most systematic analysis of the nearly half century of poll data on confidence and related questions, conclude that "the results suggest that the American people feel increasingly powerless."[33]

The poll questions that come closest to supplying information about people's feelings about their power ask in various ways whether public officials or government act in their interest. Such questions have been asked for over 40 years, and a majority of respondents usually answers that officials do not act in their interest. In effect, poll respondents are also saying that government is not responsive to them.[34]

The responsiveness questions come in various versions each of which sheds a slightly different light on what government is unresponsive about and why. One question asks respondents whether government "is pretty much run by a few big interests looking out for themselves or for the benefit of all the people." Other questions have respondents agreeing or disagreeing that "people like me don't have any say about what the government does;" that "elected officials in Washington lose touch with the people pretty quickly;" "do not care about them;" and are "not really interested in the problems of the average man."[35]

Majorities of the people being polled thought government to be reasonably responsive in the 1960s, but their feelings turned negative in the 1970s and became more negative from then on. The answers to most versions of this question hit bottom in the early 1990s and then turned slightly more positive by the end of that decade, most likely because the economy was beginning to blossom.[36]

Nonetheless, a majority of people still had their doubts. In a summer 2001 poll, 68 percent of those polled thought the views of the majority of citizens should have a great deal of influence on the decisions of Washington's elected and other officials, but only 9 percent thought that this majority actually had a great deal of influence.[37] Perhaps not by accident, a Beltway sample of public officials studied in 1998 agreed with them, more than half believing government to be "unresponsive."[38]

All the now-expected findings went by the boards just after 9/11, however, when 55 percent of those polled suddenly trusted the government to do what is right again. This is the highest percentage since the 1970s.[39] At the time, that figure probably meant that poll respondents were supporting the government's fight against terrorism without necessarily trusting it about other issues. In fact, by mid-2002, as fears of further acts of terrorism began to decline and significant numbers of Americans started worrying about the state of the economy, the schools, health insurance and the like, the levels of trust and confidence in business, government, and other major institutions began to decline once more.

Pollsters have never asked their respondents how public officials are unresponsive, and why. Consequently, clues have to be sought from a variety of related questions. Many people evidently believe elected officials pay too much attention to their peers,[40] but if they were compelled to care about their constituents, they could agree on solutions for the public's problems.[41] Caring surely has its limits, but when 9/11 suddenly reduced the public's problems down to the least common denominator, the responsiveness numbers went up accordingly.

Poll Results in Context

People's answers to pollster questions must be evaluated in the context of larger patterns in poll responses. To start, the results of the confidence studies suggest that the popular lack of confidence is not limited to business, labor, or government, but extends to many other major institutions: the news media, the medical system, banks, the military, and the law.[42] The emergence of conflict or controversy is usually enough for people to lose confidence in such institutions. Organized religion, once a major source of institutional confidence, had suffered this fate even before the sexual offenses of members of the Catholic priesthood made the headlines.

In addition, answers to many different questions, even unrelated ones, follow a common trend; high levels of trust and confidence existed in the government and other major institutions during the 1950s and 1960s, then a long downward trend begin in the 1970s that reversed itself only in the mid-1990s, and then only slightly.

Again, no one has asked poll respondents the questions to explain this trend. One guess is that people answer questions positively during periods of economic health and relatively conflict-free politics.[43] From the perspective of the general public, the country was economically healthy and politically peaceful in the 1950s and 1960s—enough so that the traumatic events of the latter half of the 1960s did not show up in the polls, or not until the 1970s. The downward turn in the 1970s may have reflected popular reactions to the antiwar and ghetto protests, the government's dishonesty about the Vietnam war and Watergate—and above all the country's concurrent economic decline, for the critical responses to the standard poll questions began with the 1973 oil crisis.[44]

The answers turned more positive with the return of prosperity in the mid-1990s, but only slightly so, the presumption being that the cultural and other "wars" of the last quarter century may have had a more lasting dampening effect.[45] How poll respondents will respond in the future cannot now even be guessed. While economic problems, and sharp political or cultural conflict will always reduce confidence, wars and other events that suppress conflict are likely to have a positive effect on confidence.

The public confidence reported in the 1960s should not be overestimated, however. Public opinion polls date back only to the late 1930s, and the handful of polls conducted between then and the 1960s suggest that popular skepticism about politics and politicians is, as historians have long told us, virtually as old as the country itself. Thus, in one early poll, in 1943, 48 percent of respondents agreed that no one could stay honest after going into politics. By 1997, the proportion had increased only slightly, to 55 percent.[46]

Another, but very different, pattern in poll responses, demonstrated by many studies over the years, is that people are inclined to feel negative about national institutions in general, but can concurrently be positive about specific ones.[47] Thus, a Pew Center study indicated that unfavorable attitudes toward the government were balanced by favorable ones toward a range of specific federal agencies, the only overwhelmingly disliked one being the Internal Revenue Service.[48]

Similarly, respondents lack confidence in the public school system but like their local schools. They feel very negative about Congress, but they are positive about their own congresspersons—one reason so many incumbents are constantly being reelected. Even the news media are affected by this pattern, television news-viewers rating the often-maligned local television news as more believable than all the national news programs other than CNN.[49]

The pattern behind this set of answers has been called "distancing," because poll respondent answers vary with the their distance (spatial, social, or other) from the subjects being researched. As in the case of the just-mentioned local school and congressional representative, respondents almost always have more faith in closer institutions and people than distant ones. This is nicely illustrated by an August 1995 Gallup poll, in which 60 percent reported feeling that the federal government had too much power, but only 27 percent and 17 percent felt that way about their state and local governments respectively.[50]

Sometimes, confidence in the local may simply be confidence in the familiar. For example, despite the great and continuing fear of crime in much of the last quarter century, the proportion of people feeling safe in their own neighborhoods has not changed significantly during that period. People's fears seem to be limited to crime elsewhere. Unfortunately, no one has asked what people fear "elsewhere" and what exactly strikes them as dangerous about the unknown.[51]

The question is important for it can involve not only fear but anger and demonization, all feelings with potentially ominous political effects. Consequently, further questions need to be asked to understand these poll results, particularly whether the feelings are about some abstract or symbolic "other" or about specific populations who are thought to be threatening.

Distrust around the World

Americans' negative feelings about their political institutions and leaders are not unique; the same findings are reported in all countries where similar questions have been asked. For example, 41 percent of European poll respondents in five Western European countries say that they "basically trust the state;" as compared to 40 percent in the United States. Only 7 percent of the Europeans and 9 percent of the Americans agreed "completely" that the "government is really run for the benefit of all the people."[52]

The European figures are based on only a few surveys, but they suggest that distrust of the government, or of the elites running it, or both, may be typical of large representative democracies dominated by big organizations, even if the countries are in some respects structured quite differently. In any case, American feelings about government unresponsiveness and related subjects can probably not be explained by distinctively American conditions.

Disempowerment: What Do People Do?

"Do people feel disempowered?" Poll data must always be taken with a grain of salt, but enough evidence exists to suggest that except for the people with direct access to the seats of power, the answer is "yes." Many would probably add that they are not interested in power. What they want, they might say, is a responsive government, or, at least responsiveness from the specific government agencies and public officials from whom they need something.

Even so, disempowerment breeds discouragement, and people who are always eager to gripe about government remain passive, as discouraged people often do. However, they are passive also because their really meaningful lives take place elsewhere, in a very different world from local and national governments and politics. This is one reason why many citizens are so hard to reach in election campaigns.

In fact, the widespread popular discomfort extends to many organized groups and once more, people shun those they do not need. Instead, they live mainly in the already mentioned informal groups which are unorganized and consist of people who trust each other. In these unorganized groups, they hope to find whatever assistance they need, along with support and other social and emotional satisfactions.

Even so, and perhaps because of America's faith in self-reliance, too few people realize how much they depend on government for their everyday lives. Actually, people can have faith in self-reliance precisely because government supplies a variety of essential but generally invisible infrastructures that support everyday life and make it possible. The supports are so invisible that people complain the moment they are withdrawn. Government has built the roads that make a commuting society possible, and it has gone to great lengths, including wars, to keep the gasoline flowing, which is why people complain the moment gasoline prices go up or waiting lines at gas stations lengthen unduly.

Despite the publicity given to popular dissatisfaction with government, more people probably complain more often about their workplaces and employers than about government and politicians. Some of the complainants may even be aware that they are more powerless in the economy than in the polity.

Nonetheless, Americans are more critical of government than of business. They regularly object to higher taxes but with some exceptions, rarely say anything when businesses raise prices. They believe government to be wasteful but they appear to assume that business is never wasteful.[53]

Maybe people still feel that government is theirs and private enterprise is not and therefore set higher standards for government and are more upset when it does not meet them. Perhaps business, or at least the sellers of goods and services, is more often responsive to people than government, since their profits depend on keeping their customers and their goodwill. Government, having a monopoly on most of the services it supplies directly to citizens, can ignore or antagonize them more easily.

The exception is at election time, when all the big guns of government come forward to plead their causes and make their promises, temporarily turning politics into a realization of the American Dream. Maybe this exception even proves a rule: that modern political systems are so complicated and in some ways so fragile that they cannot make permanent room for an unorganized and unwieldy collectivity like the citizenry. Sporadic changes of opinion, occasional protests, and the periodic demands of temporarily mobilized groups can perhaps be accommodated, but most of the time, organizations will be able to wield the greatest influence on public officials.

Still, exceptions do leave an opportunity to create a stronger role for citizens. If their ideals have any bearing on the journalists' work, they should welcome opportunities to stand up for their citizen audience. As the next two chapters will suggest, however, journalists have their own problems to solve and obstacles to overcome. For them, the ideal will have to remain just that, at least until they can cope with their own sources of disempowerment.

CHAPTER 2

Journalism and Its Troubles

As a profession, journalism views itself as supporting and strengthening the roles of citizens in democracy. Many individual journalists undoubtedly feel the same way, reflecting the ideals of their profession but in addition, informing citizens so they can play their democratic roles is the journalists' work and source of income as well.

However, journalists are employed professionals working for mainly commercial news media that try to supply what the news audience will accept and what advertisers will pay for. Much of the audience is interested in keeping up with the news rather than being politically involved citizens. These and other facts of everyday journalism complicate the profession's pursuit of its ideals.

In addition, journalists have their own troubles, and are confronting their own disempowerment. Theirs differs from that of the citizenry's because it is accompanied by a degree of professional downward mobility, brought on in part by a recent decline in usefulness. During the 1960s and 1970s, the civil rights revolution, the war in Vietnam, the antiwar protests and marches, the ghetto disorders, the Watergate scandal, and the Cold War overall, supplied the journalists with a series of major national stories that attracted a sizeable audience, and at times a greatly interested one.

In recent years, since the high points of the Gulf War and until the 9/11 tragedy and its aftermath, stories judged to be of equivalent importance to those of the past have been scarce, so news appears to play a smaller part in people's media uses. Thus, half the respondents of a 2000 Pew Center audience study reported that they followed national news only periodically, "when something important or interesting is happening."[1]

Whether yet more members of the news audience will adopt this pattern again remains to be seen, for it depends on what happens in and to the country. According to Nielsen television ratings data, the nightly audience for the three network evening news programs, which averaged around 28 million people in 2001, and was just under 27 million the week before 9/11, rose to 79 million on the day of the tragedy when the networks presented news programming around the clock.[2] The week after the tragedy, the average audience figure was about 31 million, and did not change significantly in the next six months.[3] The cable news audience grew even more dramatically. For the week after 9/11, CNN's total daily news audience, 330,000 viewers on the average, grew to nearly 3.5 million.[4] By March 2002, the total daily cable news audience stood at about 1.5 million.[5] However, by mid-2002, the audiences of the network evening news and of cable news had returned to pre-9/11 numbers.

Historically, journalists are also disempowered by changes taking place in the news industry, many of them similar to those occurring in other American industries. Shrinkage, consolidation, and conglomeration are routine events these days. Many newspapers have closed down or merged with others over the last several decades, so all but the half-dozen biggest American cities are down to one newspaper—and that one is increasingly likely to be a part of a national or regional chain such as Gannett and Knight-Ridder.[6]

In the latest installment of this trend, news firms and chains are being bought by larger corporations, including multinational conglomerates. For many of the large corporations, news is a minor part of the overall enterprise, and some may own both electronic and print firms, each of whom could also be competing with the other.[7]

A quarter century ago, a journalist, the editor-in-chief of *Time* magazine, was the head of Time, Inc. But today that same editor only heads one of several divisions of Time-Warner, an entertainment conglomerate that is itself now controlled by America Online, the internet giant.[8] A. J. Liebling's observation that "freedom of the press is guaranteed only to those who own one" needs a little updating.[9]

Starting around the 1990s, conglomerate-owned news firms, chains, and even family-owned ones, began to demand a higher rate of profit. National news media profits are not often reported separately from the companies in which they are embedded, but local news media have almost always earned well and considerably more than other firms supplying daily necessities.[10] Local television news departments report profit rates as high as 40 to 50 percent. Newspapers' earnings are somewhat more modest, currently around 20 to 25 percent in major markets, but some American newspapers have reported 30 percent profits.[11] True, profits go down too, particularly when advertisers must cut back, as they often do in bad economic times, including the recession that began in 2000. Print news media profits also decline when the price of newsprint goes up, but they go back up when that price comes down again, as it usually does.

The corporate pressure for higher profit in news firms does not differ much from that of other firms in the economy, and the reasons are not dissimilar either. The demand may be the result of shareholder pressure, the Wall Street dictate to keep up with share price and dividend levels in other firms, and management fears of a hostile takeover if Wall Street standards are not met. Undoubtedly, unexpected opportunities to increase profit and simple corporate greed may also be at play—and top executives who take home multimillion-dollar salaries and stock options can be found as well.[12] Moreover, increases in profit are likely to raise Wall Street and shareholder expectations even further, a spiral that affects news firms as much as all others.

Given the oddities of real-world capitalism, the pressure for rising news media profits did not abate with the 2000 recession and its accompanying downturn in business. That downturn was caused by the further shrinkage of the news audience, its inability or unwillingness to buy advertised goods, and the resulting reductions in advertising revenue. The result, or one of them, is yet further cost reduction and journalistic downsizing.

Another common reaction to audience shrinkage is to add "style" and other "soft" news sections in the hope of attracting, or at least maintaining, more readers or viewers and advertisers. The expansion of soft news means more jobs for feature writers who cover the medical or home design beats, and less work for reporters chasing "hard" political or disaster news. Local news media often turn to the soft news output of national news media syndicates instead of depending on local journalists.

The biggest changes have taken place in network television news, where foreign news has been cut back further and many foreign news bureaus have been eliminated.[13] A one-person bureau may cover an entire continent, the sole reporter gaining temporary reinforcements when important news develops in one of his or her areas.[14] Independent news services may provide videotape much like the print media syndicates that supply print news stories. Network television even reduced its staff of national correspondents, now relying on local reporters to cover nearby stories of national interest, with network journalists sometimes adding national voice-overs to local videotape. Now that lightweight videotape equipment and other labor-saving technologies are available, the old three-person camera crews have turned into one-person crews, the reporter assuming the camera work, sound, and all.

With the arrival of video phones, a single reporter can put live news directly on the air. This latest new technology has already enabled journalists to provide instant live coverage of the war in Afghanistan and the Middle East conflict and is likely to be used widely in the future to cover breaking news everywhere.

Control and Status Reductions

Profit pressures and budget reductions in the news media have also affected journalists' control over the news and their professional autonomy in shaping it.

One effect, which also takes place when news firms face higher profit demands, is a breakdown of the long-standing walls between "church" (the editorial side of the enterprise) and "state" (the business side). The typical breaching of the walls takes place when marketing and advertising executives ask editors and other news executives to pay more attention to the commercial needs of the firms.

As journalists see it, however, church is sacred and trumps state; editorial decision making must be totally divorced from commercial considerations and even an informal chat between commercial executives and editorial ones can sometimes be perceived as unjustifiable business interference. In many news firms, editors and television producers still do not know what ads and commercials will accompany the news. Of course editors and producers know what kinds of stories will likely sell newspapers and magazines and increase ratings, and both understand when these must be used.

Editors and producers also know that they need to maintain friendly relations with the business executives. Still, they resent hints from these executives to keep the commercial needs of the firm in mind and reserve the right to decide what stories they will supply to the news audience.

If pollster questions on this subject are reliable and valid, so far the majority of journalists do not seem particularly worried about the level of business interference. Nearly two-thirds of national journalists and half of local ones say that corporate owners have "not very much" influence on news organizations or none at all.[15]

In the national news media, business executives try instead to provide information that helps both church and state. For example, in some news firms, business departments attempt to inform journalists about their audience in the hope that journalists will cater to audience preferences when possible. News executives rarely conduct audience research, however, and while they may review the audience research undertaken by advertising departments, they do not feel obliged to share it with their news staffs. They are professionals who can and must choose whatever news they feel the citizen audience needs.[16]

Judging by their conferences, professional debates, and stories as well as editorials in their trade and professional journals, journalists seem to be especially concerned over the replacement of the family firm and small (also family-owned) chain by large chains and even larger communication conglomerates that combine entertainment and news firms into one giant corporation. Many perceive the increasing size of the firms as a major threat to their autonomy. They also appear to have a soft spot for family ownership, assuming that families are as much concerned about the public service they can perform as for the profits they can obtain.

If they have to work for chains or larger organizations, journalists believe that their professional autonomy is safer in firms in which the major decision makers are journalists rather than business professionals. In the journalistic worldview, business executives are guilty of being "bean counters" until proven innocent. Even worse are former journalists who become owners or top executives and interfere in editorial affairs to pursue economic or political agendas. This is a major problem in Europe, where some media firm owners have became major political figures, and one of whom, Silvio Berlusconi, is currently the Italian prime minister. In America, Rupert Murdoch has used some of the American media outlets he owns for political advocacy, but that he or any other top news media executive would run for political office in the United States seems unlikely.[17]

Will the journalists' beliefs and fears about the threats to their professional autonomy turn out to be accurate? Family-owned firms can put journalists in charge, but they can also be run by autocratic family members whose news judgments take priority over those of journalists, or who are out to maximize the firm's operating income, obtain unreasonable profits, or sell the business for the highest possible capital gains.[18]

Chains and conglomerates may follow the same two conflicting sets of policies, but the verdict is still out regarding which kind of news firm is more respectful of journalistic values. Conglomerates and family firms alike quickly expand their news operations when national disasters strike, sometimes spending millions of dollars of potential profits or even forfeiting advertising to give priority to a big story. The 9/11 tragedy and the war that followed are only the latest example.

Defenders of media conglomerates and chains sometimes argue that only firms of their size can afford the dramatic increases in news budgets needed to cover wars and other big stories, and in the long run this may be true. In the short run, all news firms feel some obligation to demonstrate their dedication to public service, especially since such demonstrations also maintain their reputations and competitive positions, and supply them with additional goodwill. Consequently, although budgets expand to meet public service and commercial needs, smaller firms, be they chains or family-owned, must undoubtedly cap spending before big firms feel the need to do so. In the contemporary equivalent of the Thirty Year War, were it to happen, only the giant news firms would probably survive.

Some journalists and media critics fear that in the long run, the conglomerates will not only homogenize the news but also slant it to supply favorable publicity for the other firms in the conglomerate. This fear is reasonable, but so far little evidence exists to justify it. Media conglomerates can and do use their control of print and electronic news media to publicize, recycle, and otherwise make money from commonly owned products. Until now, interlocking money-making opportunities have been exploited within the various entertainment companies, but such opportunities may not exist in the news companies. Moreover, the profit potential of news is much more limited.

Additionally, although Disney owns ABC and thus ABC News, it is unlikely to give up valuable goodwill by overtly interfering with or censoring ABC journalists. Covert censorship may be somewhat easier but because it is hard to keep secret, it remains a risky activity for an image-conscious enterprise. If one part of Disney makes a misstep, other parts of Disney may suffer too.

The extent to which journalists employed by the communication conglomerates censor themselves, consciously or not, more frequently or differently from their peers in other news firms, might tell us a lot about the dangers of conglomerates. For now, chain and corporate owners' main concerns have involved how their journalists have covered corporate corruption, internal conflicts at headquarters, and moral missteps by company bigwigs. Despite the fact family owners feel more pressure to protect their public images, even conglomerates run the risk of forefeiting goodwill if attempts to suppress news of company malfeasance becomes public knowledge.[19] Manufacturing and other large corporations that do not sell goods or services directly to consumers may be less concerned with consumers' goodwill, but such firms are also less likely, at least now, to purchase or create news divisions.

The crucial question about chains and conglomerates as opposed to traditional news firms is profit: how much profit are the news firms expected to deliver, and what effects do the pursuit and expenditure of profit have on the journalists? The more profit the firm demands, the less money is available to be spent on journalists and news coverage, the more bureaus have to be closed and the more shortcuts taken. Admittedly, firms could use extra profits to hire more journalists to improve their product and thus to earn yet higher profits, but better journalism, as defined by journalists, is not necessarily profitable. If it were, more newspapers would resemble the *New York Times* or the *Washington Post*.

In any case, increased profit demands may currently be more dangerous for journalists and their ability to report the news as they see fit, than whether their bosses are family members or corporate shareholders. Likewise, the size of the corporate owner or even the number of large owners in the relevant industry is less important than how much profit is being sought.

During an economic recession, conglomerates and big corporations may have more resilience than family news firms, but they may also require their news divisions to help rescue other parts of their enterprises. Usually, however, the news divisions are neither large nor profitable enough to become the cash cows for a sick conglomerate.

Even so, journalists may turn out to be more vulnerable in corporate than in family enterprises. For example, corporate acquisitions and reorganizations, especially those involving overhead reductions, can have indirect editorial consequences. Conglomerate top executives may treasure the news firms they have taken over, and economy-of-scale policies would instead call for the elimination of ancillary departments. Merging payroll and related departments may not matter journalistically, but when news media legal departments are closed, corporate lawyers who are unfamiliar with news media practices may take over. Being governed by conglomerate considerations, they may not defend the journalists against censorship demands and advertiser pressure as vigorously or expertly as lawyers specializing in news. Nonetheless, large family firms are not immune from similar economies.

Perhaps the most depressing consequence of profit-driven editorial cutbacks is their relative invisibility. Public officials might complain if they obtain less publicity as a result of such cutbacks, but audiences cannot know that investigative reporting, being expensive, is often cut back first when budgets are decreased. Journalists may feel that their democratic mission to go below the radar is impaired, but they have no one to whom to complain except each other.

Whatever form they take, all of state's intrusions into church are viewed not only as reductions of the journalists' control over the news, but also of their professional status. The profession's prestige outside the newsroom was never very high. Not so long ago, journalists were considered to be ink-stained wretches and bribe-taking scribblers recently emerged from the working class. Now virtually all have college degrees and many beat reporters, especially for national media, also have graduate degrees.

Nonetheless, journalists' salaries remain modest, below those of other employed professionals. National and big-city news media, which get most of the media publicity, pay many of their journalists well: salaries ranging from $150,000–200,000 are not unheard of.[20] Television pays more than the print media, and network television anchormen (although not many anchorwomen) receive, like other star performers, multimillion-dollar salaries. Conversely, small town newspaper reporters may still start at salaries of less than $25,000 a year.

Some Programmatic Consequences

Journalistic disempowerment has also crept into the formats in which news is packaged and disseminated. One major change has been the partial replacement or supplementation of "hard" news with "soft" news. Hard news typically refers to the political and related news that journalists believe citizens need to perform their democratic duties.[21] Thomas Patterson is more specific: "Hard news refers to coverage of breaking events involving top leaders, major issues, or significant disruptions in the routines of daily life, such as an earthquake or airline disaster . . . important to citizens' ability to understand and respond to the world of public affairs. News that is not of this type is, by definition, soft."[22]

Soft news is thus a very heterogeneous residual category, including human interest, scandal, entertainment, and the celebrity stories that now appear even in the most elite newspapers. Another, if sometimes less bitterly criticized form of soft news is the feature story that provides people with helpful information for everyday life, for example about heart attack prevention, healthy diets, and new lifestyles and leisure activities that are thought to enhance the quality of life. In fact, stories about health and disease are now television news staples, appearing virtually every day, and often immediately after the day's national and international news.

Journalists expect, as an integral part of their professional identities to provide hard news, so the proliferation of soft news is felt as a form of disempowerment and disrespect. Indeed, soft news is often called "infotainment," implying not very subtly that journalists who see themselves as responsible for democracy's health are being reduced to the level of mere entertainers.

The change in the hard/soft news ratio has taken on several forms. In the print media, the change can be seen clearly by the expansion of "back of the book" sections, for example, about subjects as varied as science and gardening. Television has no formal back of the book, but there are now fewer sections devoted to domestic and international political news.

Another version of this change has come in program formats, particularly in television. For example, the historic one-hour or half-hour news documentary series, such as "CBS Reports," which was often devoted to investigative reporting about a single subject, has been replaced by the semiweekly (or more) "news magazines" that supply a mix of hard and soft news.[23]

The other relevant format change is the proliferation of cable television talk and panel shows in which a host or a set of experts talk about news events with a changing array of guests to engage in the discussions. Guests are frequently chosen from opposing areas of expertise, elected officials from the two major political parties, or representatives of the Right and Center, the Left having long ago been banished from the mainstream news media. Some cable television, and many radio, programs try to draw audiences by being as argumentative as possible. These programs are usually hosted by high-decibel shouters, most of them politically conservative. Rush Limbaugh is currently the most famous of them.

When major news stories break, discussion and argument programming is replaced by hard news stories. These supply more detail than what is reported on the networks, and for that matter, in the handful of pages devoted to national and international news in most American newspapers.[24] The nearly month-long coverage of the 2000 post-election news may have supplied the news audience with more information about election procedures than it has ever received before. As news programs, the cable channels provide the detailed coverage for which there is no room, or audience, on the half-hour network news programs.[25] When cable news programs turn to discussion and argument, they supply television versions, broadly speaking, of newspaper op-ed articles and the letters-to-the-editor column.[26]

The contemporary mixed news and talk format began essentially with the O. J. Simpson trials and continued with the Clinton impeachment, after which cable news organizations deliberately looked for other controversial events that lent themselves to being formatted in this manner.[27] One debated whether Hillary Clinton should run for the Senate from New York; others raised questions about the deaths of Princess Diana and John F. Kennedy Jr.[28] In 2000, the top story concerned the events and controversies occurring during the 26 post-election days that decided the presidential election.[29] In 2001, apparently the only eligible subject was Representative Gary Condit and the disappearance of his intern-lover Chandra Levy. Though after 9/11 and the wars on terrorism replaced the Condit story, journalists apologized to themselves and others for having been seduced by sensationalism.

Some observers see the cable channel news programs as a public forum stimulating citizen discussion of the country's issues. Others note that they mainly provide an additional voice for establishment political figures and conservative ideologues, offering people a limited or even one-sided perspective on current events and issues. The most important question is about audience reaction, however: do these programs reach enough people to matter, and do they encourage public discussion or do they preach largely to the converted? The answers are important, for if and when cable channels, and the internet, attract most of the loyal but sophisticated "news buffs," network television news can put more energy into attracting the rest of the news audience.

Although cable news programs have, at least since 9/11, restored some of the hard news that had disappeared from the news media, many journalists place their faith in the internet. They hope that it will make possible a much larger amount of hard news coverage. However, the internet is still so new that even guesses about its future are premature.[30] Most likely, the internet will continue to supply a humongous amount of news and news-related websites of varying degrees of accuracy and credibility, but the news audience can—and will—pay attention to only a handful of outlets across all the news media. For example, a Nielsen Media Research study discovered that while TV viewers had access to over 70 channels in the year 2000, they watched only about ten of them—just about the same number they watched in 1994 when they could receive only about 40.[31] The same pattern is likely to hold for the internet, and because almost all the mainstream news media already have well-attended websites, they are likely to play a dominant role in internet news at least for the foreseeable future.[32]

Today's major news websites are near-copies, often abbreviated, of the print and television versions, with added links and archives to serve news buffs wanting more detail. In fact, the internet provides the most abbreviated news in all the news media, which may help explain why many young people, who are traditionally the least interested in the news, are getting most of their news from the web.

Someday print and electronic media may be entirely replaced by websites (or future versions thereof), but even so, news media can exist only if they include news organizations.[33] Without them they are something other than news media.

Disempowerment by Audience Shrinkage

The news audience participates in the disempowerment of the news media mainly by disappearing, at least judging by declining circulation and ratings numbers. Audience loss not only chips away at the economic base of news firms, but it is a primary cause of the closing of newspapers and other, mostly print, news media and the downsizing of news staffs.

Daily newspapers have been losing circulation ever since the end of World War II. The news magazines have not suffered drastic losses in readers, but their circulations have not grown proportionately with the increasing American population.

Concurrently, the remaining audience has cut down on its consumption of print media news. For example, a Pew Center study reported that "yesterday's" reading of the newspaper declined from 71 percent of the respondents in 1965 to 52 percent in 1995 and to 45 percent in 2000, although the numbers have always risen temporarily when important events are taking place.[34]

Moreover, all print news media have lost audience to television over the years. Still, the ratings of the television network news programs have also declined more or less steadily since about the 1970s, and even local television news, always the most popular, began to see its audience shrink in the 1990s.[35]

Actually, the standard data about the still-loyal news audience may overstate its attention to the news. Whether people buy newspapers or even say they read them does not supply information about whether and how much they are reading the news pages. Turning on TV news programs provides no data on whether people are paying attention. Many people now watch TV news with the remote control in hand, 62 percent of the Pew Center respondents indicating that they did so in 2000.[36] In fact, news producers assume, although not necessarily correctly, that their viewers will use the remote control the moment their interest flags.

Conversely, it is not even certain that the news audience has been shrinking, as it may just be spread across more and more news outlets. As a result, three-quarters of the respondents of a Pew Center study agreed that there were "so many ways to get the news" that they did not worry about missing an issue of their paper or their "usual news program."[37] National and international news summaries are available on the many local TV news programs of stations affiliated with networks. Radio news summaries are available during the day on car radios as people commute to and from work, and innumerable websites, including major internet browsers can be checked quickly at work, at least in permissive workplaces. Further, a part of the news audience has always obtained its news indirectly, from family and friends, but no one knows how many—or where—their news sources get their news.

So little is known about the news audience that multiple explanations can be suggested for what people are doing. For example, the decline in the newspaper and television news audience, and the dispersion of the audience across a number of news media could suggest that people are switching from *long* news to *short* news. For habitual "keeping up" they may be relying on short news summaries and bulletins on television, in the newspapers, the internet and elsewhere, returning to longer newspaper, magazine, and television news stories when events warrant. Nonetheless, a 2002 Pew Center study indicates that 80 percent of the respondents reported getting at least some news every day.[38]

Assuming the total news audience has in fact been declining over the last two decades, it could also be interpreted as the return to a normal level of attention to the news media that was briefly increased by the series of dramatic news events in the 1960s and 1970s, starting with the climax of the civil rights movement's long years of activism and closing with the end of the Vietnam War.

An additional explanation is that the decrease in the news audience is merely part of a general and continuing decrease in the audience of all mass media, print and electronic.[39] Perhaps the age of the mass media is coming to an end: part of a larger lifestyle change having nothing to do with the news.

The lifestyle change might not even be voluntary, but a result of longer working hours by family breadwinners, who regain some of the time they need for raising children and for routine chores by cutting back on the news and other mass media fare.

Possible explanations are all very well, but reliable data to check any of them out does not exist. Circulation figures, ratings, and even poll respondents' answers to questions about their news media usage say nothing about how much people read and view, with what level of long-term comprehension, and how much they use the news to understand government, politics, and other subjects relevant to their roles as citizens. The publicly available data is too superficial to be useful.

Even if the data is subject to question, the numbers reporting decline in the news audience have to be disconcerting to journalists, making them feel they are less and less needed for traditional newsgathering. That the news audience can find news in more media more of the time is not an unalloyed positive for them either, for while audiences have always been fickle, the contemporary dispersion of the news media makes journalists feel that they must constantly pursue the audience to hold its attention. Although readers could always turn newspaper pages, or even toss the news sections unread into the garbage, the image of television news viewers with trigger fingers on their remotes is in many respects more threatening.

At least one positive note about the audience is available. If past trends that news consumption increases with age hold up, the aging of the baby boomers and the increasing proportion of older people in the total population should gladden the hearts of journalists.[40] The only trouble is that advertisers, and also the journalists themselves, would much prefer to reach an audience of younger adults.

Disempowerment by Audience Disapproval

The possible lessening of audience interest in the news is not the only problem with which journalists must cope. A second and equally disempowering problem is lack of audience confidence in the news media and unhappiness with some journalistic methods, which the American Society of Newspaper Editors (ASNE) has recently described as a problem of journalistic credibility.[41]

Actually, popular satisfaction with the news media has never been great. The confidence studies discussed in Chapter 1 also asked people about their confidence in "newspapers or the press," and found that it is no higher than in government, having followed much the same pattern of steady and only rarely interrupted decline since the 1960s.[42]

The poll respondents' dissatisfaction is not really about a lack of credibility however. Instead, inaccuracy, insufficient attention to audience concerns, or bias toward one or another political group or socioeconomic stratum are at the root of their discontent.

Inaccuracy may be the most frequently voiced criticism in studies of the news audience, but the term is used very loosely. Although people are unhappy with small inaccuracies such as misspelled names and incorrect details, particularly in local stories, they also see these as symptoms of a more serious problem: the journalists' inability to understand them.[43] When not telling the whole story is viewed as inaccuracy, the term becomes a synonym for bias.[44] In fact, the news audience regularly accuses journalists of bias, not only when their perception of the facts varies from that of the audience, but when journalists disagree among themselves about that perception.[45] Nonetheless, the audience's bias charges are not ideological and have nothing to do with the bias accusations made regularly by conservative media critics and right-wing "spokesmen" and their radical peers.

If the polls are right, citizens feel that the news media are as unresponsive to them as is government. In one of the first, or perhaps the first-published news audience survey, a 1939 *Fortune* study, nearly half of the respondents felt the newspapers soft-pedalled unfavorable news about "friendly politicians," and "friends of the publishers." Over a quarter also felt that the papers were "too friendly" toward "people of wealth" as compared to about 10 percent who said they were too friendly to labor.[46]

The 1985 and 1998 ASNE credibility studies reported the same kind of non-responsiveness: the press "looks out mainly for rich and powerful people;"[47] and is "out of touch with mainstream Americans."[48] Another poll found nearly a majority seconding a statement that journalists do not care about democracy.[49] Several studies, including the cited ones, indicate that reporters are felt to be more responsive to their editors' and their employers' points of view than to that of the news audience.[50]

The other major complaint, reflecting yet another kind of nonresponsiveness to people, was journalistic intrusion into people's private lives for the sake of a story, particularly after a family tragedy, and when journalists ask victims, "How do you feel?" This criticism has appeared in surveys and stories by media critics for a long time.[51]

Further objections to journalistic intrusiveness include reporters not identifying themselves and recording people without telling them. Poll respondents object less often if the story is the result of investigative reporting of private or public wrongdoing, however.[52] As in several of the studies reported in Chapter 1, respondents are generally unhappy about political and other conflict, preferring, for example, that investigative reporting end up with solutions rather than exposés.[53]

Pollster studies of how respondents feel about the news media are, of course, saddled with the same uncertainties as those reported in the previous chapter. For example, general questions about journalists and their practices are typically answered more negatively than questions about specific practices or specific news media.[54]

The similarity of people's feelings about the government and the news media is surely no accident, but once more the poll data cannot offer an explanation. One possibility is that poll respondents are reacting to both news media and government as big institutions; another is that unhappiness about the government produces some or much of the unhappiness with the news media; the normal penalty for messengers. But what if people felt more positive about government; would they then pay more attention to the news? Or would they pay even less, knowing that government is looking after their interests? Or are feelings about government or news media less important than people's need for or interest in the news?[55]

In all fairness, journalists are not unaware of their faults, and often accept their audience's criticisms, such as "being out of touch with their audience," and reporting too few stories "meaningful to average Americans."[56] They even accept blame for a news effect that the audience says it does not feel: news and information "overload."[57]

Journalists' Reactions to Their Troubles

Journalists rarely say much about their lack of power or their other troubles, and are reluctant to argue with people who criticize them.[58] Instead, they join in the criticism, a variety of journalists becoming media critics. Some are journalists who have retrained themselves to be media critics. Others are nationally well known—or retired—journalists who have become part-time or full-time commentators about their profession. They write books or articles or columns in trade journals; and they appear at the endless round of conferences held by professional organizations, journalism schools, and others.[59] Many of these conferences are nominally about some of journalism's troubles, but often the speakers content themselves with voicing their own criticisms of journalism. Because these conferences are publicized by inviting name journalists, a good deal of the professional self-criticism comes from the journalists who are best known to the general public.

As a result, the critics and other commentators are, almost by definition, from the elite strata of the elite news media. Rank-and-file practitioners are not excluded but they are kept so busy meeting deadlines that they do not often have time to write or talk publicly about journalism. Professional organizations sometimes make statements about the profession. Academic and other institutes publish studies that include statements, as do ideologically driven organizations, one or two each from the Left and the Right.[60] These organizations are small although the right-wing ones are supported, and generously so, by several of the major conservative and ultra-conservative foundations, such as the Heritage Foundation and the Scaife Foundation.

What all these voices have to say about the condition of contemporary journalism requires a separate study, but an impressionistic overview suggests that journalists react to what I call disempowerment in six different ways.

Critiquing the Outsiders   As already indicated, journalists have developed their own version of the more general economic critique, which emphasizes their reaction to the takeover of news firms by chains and conglomerates that are driving out family firms. However, the commentators seem to pay as much attention to the transfer of control from journalists to nonjournalists as to the economic changes.[61] They write approvingly of family firms mainly because these are often headed by journalists or appoint news executives who are journalists.[62]

Self-Study   A second reaction is professional self-study, in which researchers or experts, in or hired by, a journalistic organization look at journalism to see whether and how it might have contributed to its troubles. Other self-studies have sought to find out what the news audience thinks of journalists, or feels about journalistic practices that have come under criticism. Two sets of studies, both already referred to, fall into this category. One is the ASNE series on credibility.

The other series of studies has been undertaken by a group of respected senior journalists that came together in the 1990s as the Committee of Concerned Journalists. The committee has published a number of evaluations, for example of the much-criticized local television news program and of several of America's newspapers.[63]

However, the committee's prime self-study project so far has been the previously noted Pew Center survey of journalists,[64] which found among other things, that when asked by pollsters, journalists continue to support the traditional values of their profession.[65] Whether and when the competitive pressures of the profession force journalists to jettison these values in their everyday work awaits further research.

The other product of the committee has been the already-cited text *Elements of Journalism*, a sterling restatement and discussion of the ideals of the profession. The authors view the ideals as, among other things, a weapon with which to fight the commercial and other forces threatening the profession, but whether any ideal has sufficient fire power to overcome a powerful reality is doubtful.

Public Journalism   While some critics of the profession seek a rededication to professional ideals, others have been trying to strengthen journalistic commitment to political education and democracy. The main vehicle has been public or civic journalism, a professional reform movement that began in the 1980s and has now grown into a multifaceted set of projects to advance local, usually small city, democracy.[66]

The projects themselves vary widely. Most are pegged to forthcoming elections, experimenting with new ways to inform the citizenry. Others develop new news formats to stimulate voting and other kinds of citizen participation, or to increase voter interest in and candidates' attention to "the issues." For example, a few newspapers have tried to reorganize their local news pages and the categories and sections in which political news is reported. In some cases, local news media have even held community meetings to supply relevant political information and to encourage feedback from politicians to citizens. Indeed, public journalism has received so much attention that by now it is being used as a label to justify a large variety of projects, including some that intentionally or otherwise try to replace politics with non-adversarial civics. A few newspapers have been criticized for using public journalism to strengthen publisher-business community alliances, or to build circulation.[67]

So far, public journalism has been attempted mainly by newspapers, and particularly those in small and middle-sized towns. Big city and national newspapers have not participated, and some of their editors have spearheaded the opposition to public journalism, seeing the movement as a threat to journalism's objectivity and autonomy and crossing the line that separates journalism from politics.

Audience Shortcomings   Another response to disempowerment blames the news audience for what is perceived as its lack of interest in "serious" (read: hard) news and for its unhealthy interest in what the journalists call "infotainment."[68] The journalists' unhappiness with infotainment reflects their view that news is either hard or soft, and that soft news unconnected to hard news must be entertainment. Thus, any information that journalists believe can titillate, divert, and distract the audience, or allows it to escape from the reality depicted by hard news, is dismissed as infotainment.

The absence of data about the motives that drive the news audience enables journalists to assume blameworthy audience motives, but entirely different assumptions are also possible. Thus, it is hard to imagine that anyone in the news audience found talk shows discussing the deaths of Princess Diana and John Kennedy titillating, or those considering O. J. Simpson's trials for murder—and his guilt or innocence—diverting.

In fact, stories about celebrity deaths and similar tragedies that journalists condemn as infotainment can give audience members an opportunity to feel sympathy for victims and anger at villains.[69] Such stories remind people that elites are no more spared from tragedies than ordinary people.[70] These reminders could also induce a false identification with elites; or conversely, the satisfaction that elites are being punished for the power and privilege that come with high status. None of these reactions can be considered entertainment.

Celebrity gossip may not belong in the same news pages as hard news, but unless it is sheer puffery, such gossip may also help the audience feel morally superior, and it, like scandal, relegitimates social norms and restates mainstream definitions of normal behavior. Even "reality programming" has some informational virtues. Although clearly intended to titillate and distract, these programs may also demonstrate how to maneuver in and through competitive social situations of the kind that many people face frequently, notably in the workplace. Although a documentary on dealing with unreasonable superiors and bullies at work might supply more information, programs like "Survivor" may communicate similar information to the people who do not watch or learn from documentaries. Admittedly, stories about individuals dealing with workplace bullies are not hard news, but I suspect that many members of the news audience may want such news more than they want hard news stories about the secretary of state dealing with international bullies.

The media critics' obsession with infotainment may express the profession's belief that it is failing to educate its audience in citizenship, and failing democracy by its inability to persuade the audience to give priority to hard news. However, some journalists may feel that they are losing status by having to report what they call infotainment, just as some of their professional ancestors objected to similar stories reported by the "yellow press" or the tabloids.

Criticism of Fellow Professionals   A fifth reaction to the loss of journalistic status and power is the criticism of colleagues for excessive ambition and greed, which further reduces the camaraderie between journalists and their audience thought to have existed in the past.[71]

One target of this criticism are "celebrity journalists," notably the anchorpersons, hosts, and commentators of television news, columnists in major newspapers and magazines, and other highly visible national journalists. Their names appear in gossip columns and society pages, they are photographed with movie stars at charity benefits, and their houses and vacation retreats are occasionally featured in architectural magazines.[72]

The number of celebrity journalists is tiny, but unlike virtually all of their colleagues, they are very visible.[73] Their visibility, and more importantly, their pay and status are thought to disable them from working in a profession that requires detachment and objectivity, both of which are thought to be facilitated by invisibility.[74] Their high status brings them together with other people of high status, prompting the fear that they might view the country as if it were populated largely by other Americans with seven-figure salaries.[75] Perhaps celebrity journalists harbor that fear themselves, for many wish they were less visible so that they could occasionally become reporters again.

The most widely criticized celebrities, however, are journalists who accept large honoraria on the lecture circuit, typically to address corporate or trade association meetings. Journalist lecturers may someday have to interview members of these associations for a news story, especially an investigative one.[76] The resulting conflict of interest, potential and actual, has led many news organizations to ban such practices, but enough profitable speech-making opportunities continue to keep the criticism alive.[77]

Another high-status target is the handful of political celebrities: former elected officials and high-level political staffers who become journalists. They function typically as hosts or interviewers on talk and panel shows, and many eventually go back into politics. Perhaps the best known is Patrick Buchanan who moved between journalism and presidential candidacy in the 1990s. The entry of former politicians into the news media is another example of the commercial attractiveness of previously visible public figures, but it is also an effect of journalism's historic openness to workers without professional training. Even so, journalists consider ex-politicians to be colleagues only if and when they have completely shed their political functions and allegiances.[78]

The objection to celebrity journalists and others who become very rich and famous is connected to and partly justified by the belief that once upon a time, journalists were ordinary workers serving, and socially close to, a primarily working-class news audience. Upward mobility has created a socioeconomic gap between journalists and audience that some journalists think helps explain audience disinterest in the news.

The image of the journalist as low-status "scribbler" was disseminated in plays, novels, and movies of the 1930s and 1940s but it has also been incorporated into the collective memory of the profession's actual past.[79] Whether this collective memory is based on fact is another question, for which reliable evidence is unavailable.

Until about the last half century, journalism was not a prestigious craft, and undoubtedly a significant number of journalists once came, like most Americans, from rural or working-class homes.[80] In addition, until the arrival of mass-circulation newspapers, journalism was insecure enough work to be seen, according to one study, as a way station to "politics, business, literature or editorial work."[81] Even so, journalism did not seem to attract working-class people, and if journalists viewed themselves as industrial workers, they did not live among such workers.[82] A 1971 study of journalists showed that just about half were children of managers or professionals.[83] Fifty-eight percent of these journalists had attended or graduated from college.[84]

Perhaps journalists were once closer to their news audience, culturally and in spirit, than now, but if so, I would imagine that most were or felt closer to their middle-class than their working-class audience.[85] A larger number of the journalists of the past may have been more radical or liberal than today's, again at least in the cities, but then so were more of their readers.

Whether urban newspapers themselves were once closer to their audiences than today is doubtful. There is little evidence that except for some big city tabloids, their pages were once dominated by working-class values. In fact, perhaps because the journalists of the past were not viewed as professionals, those not protected by unions were under the thumbs of their publishers to a greater extent than now.

In addition, the publishers were often major business figures in the community, rather than professionals or managers trying to hold on to their readers and advertisers. When Franklin D. Roosevelt ran for the presidency he could count on most newspapers to endorse his opponents, as about three-fourths of all newspaper publishers were Republicans. Most are still Republican today, but political endorsements are now frequently made by editors or editorial page editors, and they may support Democrats.

"Declinism"   Journalism's final reaction to its disempowerment is "declinism," the perception that the profession that had just experienced a golden age is now in decline.[86] Although declines have obviously taken place, in budgets, audiences, and the number of news organizations among other attributes, declinism views these as part of a more general trend that signifies a largely bleak future for the profession. Not all journalists are beset by declinism, and some of the pessimism that accompanies declinism is justified, but the overall reaction interferes with thinking about a more positive future.

The golden age idealized in the journalistic imagination lasted from the 1960s to the mid-1970s, although for older journalists, that age began during World War II when now-fabled journalists such as Edward R. Murrow and the "Murrow boys" were at work.

Like all golden ages, the journalists' is a mixture of empirical fact and nostalgic imagination.[87] According to the most prevalent version, news became a national necessity during the most recent golden age. Today's half-hour network evening news programs that began in 1962, quickly demonstrated the attractions of filmed news stories, and just as quickly amassed an immense audience.[88] Network news anchormen like Walter Cronkite and "Huntley-Brinkley" (Chet Huntley and David Brinkley), were at the helm of the new news medium and were admired and respected as journalists but were not yet treated like celebrities.

In part because television news supplied prestige to the networks, their executives doled out generous budgets to their news divisions, established documentary divisions, and did not demand intense competition for audiences. However, the status and credibility of journalists were high in all of the news media then, and neither reporters nor editors (and producers) had to worry about circulation, ratings, or commercial demands from the business side.

This golden age, and similar golden ages among the print news media, are not entirely imaginary. But the past was not quite as glorious as its current journalistic conception. Today's big chains were just starting in earnest to buy up newspapers, but even then the papers themselves were losing circulation and some were going under.

The half-hour network television news came into being not in response to popular demand for news or corporate enthusiasm for journalism, but as one way to repair the networks' image and credibility after the exposure of the quiz program scandal of the late 1950s.[89] Although the news programs were not required to act as profit centers, they did in fact compete for ratings as they do now, and heads rolled if ratings declined precipitously. Still, the median age of the audience for the network evening news was in the mid-50s then as it is now, and 5 percent of the total weekly audience watched the news programs daily.[90]

Perhaps most important, although not always sufficiently emphasized in the golden-age myth, the journalists of the period were able to report a long set of important and audience-attracting events, one after the other. The era of newsworthy events began with the Great Depression (insofar as that was covered) and World War II, which were followed by the Korean War, the events of the McCarthy era, the civil rights movement, the Bay of Pigs debacle, and the assassination of John F. Kennedy. It ended with Watergate and the resignation of Richard Nixon, but war news from Vietnam and the ups and downs of the Cold War were always available in between. In fact, Reuven Frank, who created NBC's half-hour evening news and produced a number of the network's early and now-classic documentaries, suggests that to the extent a golden age existed, it was made possible by the Cold War and the events connected with it.

Still, the journalists of the period did not think they were living through a golden age.[91] Most of the events that became dramatic in retrospect were then a set of logistic obstacles and financial challenges to the journalists who had to turn them into news stories. In addition, the more important or attention getting the story, the more pressure was exerted on editors and producers to rise above the competition in story quality as well as circulations or ratings. The newspapers competed with scoops, headlines, gossip, comics, sports pages, and classified ads; news magazines did so mainly with columnists and cover stories. Television news depended on its anchormen: a quarter of the audience choosing news programs chose them for their anchormen.

Golden ages are images of the past that emerge from dismay with the present and are constructed to fit the shortcomings of that present. Despite the many journalistic appeals for a return to journalism's performance during the last golden age, that return is impossible. Remembering a golden age may be emotionally satisfying, but even one that existed just the way it is remembered offers no solution to present problems.

Although celebrating the nostalgia for a golden age is comforting, the pessimism that accompanies the nostalgia is not. Consequently, journalists seem to have begun to imagine an optimistic future that compensates in part for the end of the golden age. The future is the internet; it is hoped it will enable journalism to recreate its past achievements as well as yet-unrealized goals. Whether and how future technology would be able to guarantee the occurrence of newsworthy events and audience receptivity to the news is not specified.[92]

The internet lends itself to such a hopeful revival in part because its promoters promise a constant stream of new and better technological ware. Moreover, unlike television news, which was expected to destroy all competing news media, the internet is perceived as being able to achieve the highest hopes of the older news media as well. Because internet formats effectively utilize the distinctive features of both electronic and print news, perhaps the new technology will usher in a new golden age. The fact that young people, who have a well-earned reputation for ignoring the news, are paying some attention to it on the web is seen as a good omen for the future. As a result, journalism schools, research centers, and conference conveners, among others, expend a considerable amount of energy and funds to explore new technology.[93] What kinds of news can be supplied and what audiences and advertisers will be drawn to it, is much harder to predict, and at this point, evidence for a golden age of internet news does not exist.[94] The history of technological innovation suggests that the cultural, social, and economic innovations expected from new technologies do not often materialize. Consequently, technology alone will do little to create a bright future for journalism.

Problems of Problem Solving

Journalists do not often pay attention to social science research to bear on their problems, but they seem to have done so enthusiastically with the research that eventuated in Robert Putnam's 2000 book *Bowling Alone*.[95] Many stories about his findings appeared in the news media when he started publishing articles, and they continued with the book's publication. In fact, he received nearly three times as many Lexis-Nexis mentions as William Julius Wilson, another much-written-about social scientist, after the publication of his book *When Work Disappears*.[96]

Putnam's main theme, the drop in organizational participation and other kinds of "civic engagement" since the 1970s, is a quintessentially declinist analysis. Moreover, the decline Putnam describes begins just about the same time as the end of the journalists' golden age. Although Putnam's analysis is supported by a great deal of empirical evidence, it assumes—and is nostalgic about—a golden age of civic virtue for which he presents no reliable evidence.[97] After 9/11, Putnam suddenly turned optimist, arguing that the war on terrorism would increase civic engagement and other kinds of participation, and that Americans would once again be bowling together.[98] A number of journalists felt likewise, believing that some of the people who left the news audience would now return and that news firms would thereafter open the budgetary spigots somewhat and reopen foreign news bureaus.

Putnam may also be popular with journalists because, like many journalists, he sees human behavior, society, and social change driven primarily by values and favors reviving those of the past. He thus strikes a chord among those journalists who hope that the profession's faith in and adherence to its traditional values will help solve journalism's problems. True, journalists also identify their problems with economic changes in the news industry and the declining audience for news, but they nonetheless hope that their professional values will see them through to a better future. One result is that journalists virtually eschew solutions beyond value change—and their books about the problems of their profession are typically short on practical solutions.[99] The focus on values also discourages attempts to think strategically about solving the problems of the profession.

Unfortunately, by now even the most subtle strategic thinking may not be enough. If the news media are going to remain under the control of news firms seeking an ever-higher profit, journalists do not have much leeway. They must either find ways of adapting journalism to produce the required profit, or figure out how to supply the news in other ways.

Their supply options are, however, restricted by demand options, for ultimately the audience, or at least that part that attracts the advertisers, generates much of the needed profit. If the audience is declining for reasons that journalists could reverse, they could aim to reinvent journalism in ways that would satisfy both audiences and themselves. If the audience is leaving for reasons the journalists cannot reverse, their reinvention needs to take a radically different direction. There may not even be satisfactory solutions, but it is much too early to come to that conclusion.

CHAPTER 3

Journalistic Practices and Their Problems

J ournalists face other obstacles in their efforts to achieve their democratic ideal. Some of these problems originate in the operating structure of the news media, resulting from the need to disseminate the news quickly, regularly, and in a highly competitive industry. Other problems stem from the democratic ideal, the values it espouses, and the disconnects between the ideal and reality.

I am sometimes critical of journalism, but first and foremost, my analysis emphasizes the structure within which journalists work. Journalistic work is almost always performed under difficult conditions of one kind or another, and most of the important imperfections—the ones with which I am mainly concerned—reside in the structures of the news media.

Of course, not all of these imperfections are to be found in all news media; some apply more to radio and television, others more to newspapers and news magazines. My overall focus is on national news media, and I write more about the more popular news media than the elite ones. Still, many observations that follow apply virtually universally, for they inhere in commercial news media and professional journalism.

An empirical study of the news media would indicate which observations apply to what news media and news outlets, but this is an essay and I take the liberty of writing about the national news media and journalism in general.

Outside and Top-Down News

From the perspective of their audience, journalists, especially national ones covering national leaders, are outsiders who are often seen, rightly or wrongly, as representatives of the elite and the world of money and power in which they travel.

These outsiders deliver news that deals mostly with people of power and high rank.[1] Thus, routine political news reports mostly on leading government officials: from the president and a few cabinet secretaries to the influential members of the House and Senate.[2] For the most part, then, political news comes to the citizenry from the top down.

That top does not reach far down, however. For example, minor cabinet departments, such as the U.S. Department of Housing and Urban Development (HUD), make the news mainly when their heads fight other cabinet officials, or when they and their agencies are charged with corruption. In HUD's case, dramatic proposals for and achievements in housing policy are reported as well, but other important housing policies get less attention than ceremonies taking place in the White House.[3]

The newsworthy cabinet departments and agencies include those in charge of national security and official violence, for example, State, Defense, and the FBI as well as the CIA. These agencies are thought newsworthy because they defend the nation, and journalists consider it their job to report on the nation. National and individual security were already of high priority before the "homeland" was attacked. Since the end of the Cold War, federal agencies relevant to banking, investment, and the global economy, notably Treasury and the Federal Reserve Bank, have become newsworthy as well, but Commerce and Labor have not. Even though there are more workers in the country than bankers, the highest officials in the Treasury and the Federal Reserve Bank regularly supply the national news about work and workers.

Top-down governmental news has many problematic consequences. For one thing, it reflects the perspective of those at the top, who tend to see the mass of the population as constituents and their society as a world they know primarily through their official capacities, and visit mainly at election time.

Moreover, the journalists respect their official sources, reporting what these sources tell them. They may be critical of what they are told and of the sources themselves, but the sources usually have the first say, thereby putting the critics in a reactive and as such inferior position. Elite news media are as respectful as others, even though they frequently give more space or time to the critics than other news media.

The need to attract an audience and to hold its attention encourages journalists to dramatize ordinary stories, but they rarely do so when they report on high officials, especially the president. Officials of course tell mostly official news, enabling them to simultaneously hide self-interested actions and justifications of their actions behind the imprimatur associated with their offices. If these officials tell lies, journalists can suggest that they have done so but only if they find other sources who allow themselves be quoted to that effect—and these are not always available. Even rarer is an official or journalist actually using the word lie; high officials usually misspeak, are misinterpreted, or quoted out of context.[4]

Thus, whether they want to or not, journalists help legitimate and even glorify the sources and strata from which they report. In effect, journalists "follow the power."[5] For example, journalists typically report the president as undertaking an action or making a statement, but they know that someone in his administration undertook the action, which the president may not even have known about. The journalists also know that statements are written by speech writers that the president sometimes sees only when they appear on his teleprompter. These practices are all customary and, having gone on for decades, are taken for granted, but they turn journalists into publicists.[6]

The degree to which the news media legitimate the president became particularly noticeable after the 2000 presidential election. Even before George Bush's election had become a fait accompli, the news media began to report policy statements emanating from the Bush camp as though he were already president.[7] The news media appeared to need a president to top their top-down news.[8] Indeed, they needed such a president badly enough that they quickly relegated further reports about Florida voting irregularities or public grumbling about stolen elections to the back news pages. The filling of the office had quickly become more newsworthy than the citizenry and whom it had chosen for president.

Part of the journalistic need was for an incumbent. In a country that so often reelects incumbents, and in the absence of intense conflict between the major parties, journalists report on incumbents because they can act and speak as officials. Except at the presidential level, challengers have to do a good bit of challenging to be heard, especially before journalists turn on the machinery that sets the coverage of primary campaigns in motion. The entire process is unintentional, but the end result is to privilege the politics of incumbency.

The principal incumbents of at least the last quarter century have been Republicans or conservative Democrats, which helps to explain why the news has become noticeably more conservative during that period.[9] The presence of these incumbents has also helped well-financed conservative groups get into the news.[10] Journalists would not find them so relevant were they not able to supplement news coming from incumbents. If liberals were in power, small and underfinanced groups that are unable to make themselves visible on their own would become more visible because they could then supply journalists with news that enhances information from incumbents.[11]

Whether incumbents are conservative or liberal, the top does not reach beyond government. As a result, top-down news excludes most economic and other elites, for even if they have unusual amounts of power in the country or the government, they are not public officials and thus rarely newsworthy. Their names only appear in the news when they or their representatives supply money during election campaigns, or later when they are White House guests, become too closely involved in government policymaking, or get into trouble with government agencies. At this writing (June 2002) the elites most in trouble with government were CEOs.

To whatever extent journalists view themselves as reporting for the democratic citizenry, they cover the news from a citizen's perspective only in a limited fashion. Journalism proceeds on the assumption that if it reports the activites of the high and mighty, citizens have the information they need to perform their democratic roles and responsibilities. The news does not take much account of the political roles that citizens themselves actually play. Despite the lip service journalists give to citizen participation, how and why people participate, other than voting, is rarely reported.

How citizens influence the actions or thinking of politicians rarely becomes newsworthy. Limited amounts of peaceful and prearranged protest will make it into the news, but if too many citizens respond enthusiastically to militant leaders or become too angry or militant themselves, the reportage is apt to be about the militancy. If citizens upset the police that are always present at citizen protests, their participation may be coded and reported as "trouble," even if the trouble does not originate with the citizens. Trouble stories always trump those reporting peaceful protests, and often peaceful protest stories are limited to the information that there was no trouble. The issues that protesters represent obtain much less attention, whether they concern global warming and other environmental issues or neighborhood fights over the retention of vacant lots for community gardens.

The distance between citizens and journalists also affects the choice of issues to be reported. Because journalists cover mainly high-level office holders, they naturally concentrate on the issues these individuals deem important. Meanwhile, journalists are too far removed from the citizenry to report, or even investigate what issues are of highest priority to them.[12] The news media rely on the pollsters, or conduct their own polls, but pollsters mainly inquire about people's opinions about the issues being considered or debated by elected officials. Researchers rarely ask citizens what upsets them or what they want.

The news media's top-down perspective generally leaves the bureaucracy out of the news, especially the agencies that are relevant to most citizens. National news cannot cover the local and lower-level officials with whom citizens have the most direct contact, but it could pay more attention to the federal agencies that deal with public and consumer issues important in everyday life. To be sure, journalists are there when federal officials report health violations by food processors, but they do not report these officials' routine activities even as they cover the routine activities of the White House.

In effect, top-down news turns journalists into messengers of the very political, governmental, and other leaders who are, as I showed in Chapter 1, felt to be untrustworthy and unresponsive by significant numbers of poll respondents. Journalists do not acknowledge, and most likely are not even aware that the news audience lacks trust in the very people and agencies about which they are reporting, and as a result, whatever connections exist between the public's lack of trust and currently newsworthy events are not considered in the news. Nobody knows whether the news media's day-to-day coverage of government and politics increases or decreases the level of public mistrust.

As the last chapter showed, the news media are themselves mistrusted by their audience and in part for a similar nonresponsiveness. How much journalists are mistrusted for their own perceived shortcomings or for reporting on mistrusted sources is worth asking.

News as Mass Production

The set of problems I have described in the previous section are not the outcome of a liberal (or conservative) journalistic ideology. Nor can they be explained as the work of journalistic serfs obeying the commands of their corporate owners.

The problems stem largely from the very nature of commercially supplied news in a big country.[13] News organizations are responsible for supplying an always new product to a large number of people, regularly and on time. As a result, news must be mass produced, virtually requiring an industrial process that takes place on a kind of assembly line.[14]

The manufacturing process usually begins with assignment editors choosing events, statements, and other phenomena that deserve to be reported. Reporters do legwork to obtain the raw materials they synthesize, with words, pictures, and videotapes, into news stories.[15]

These stories are then sorted and checked to make sure they meet the organization's quality standards. They go first to middle-level managers, that is, editors or producers, who then pass them on to the top editors or producers, who choose the final stories to be assembled into newspapers, magazines, and electronic news programs.[16] Ultimately, the stories go to a variety of technicians who oversee the machines that now do most of the literal manufacturing and distributing of the final news product to its customers.

News organizations can thus be compared to factories. Their products are manufactured as cheaply as possible, but with sufficient distinctiveness to make them competitive with others. Car makers compete mainly with each other, while journalists also have to compete with entertainers.

In addition, competition is so intense that, thanks to the invention of various new electronic media, journalists must now produce a constantly changing product. Newspapers were and are usually distributed in two or three editions a day. But television news must be updated for every news program, and internet journalists never stop updating, whether the news website is that of a major search engine or the *New York Times*. What is called the perpetual news cycle therefore requires, more than ever before, that a fresh product be manufactured in the fastest, most routinized, and efficient way possible.

Speed was essential even in the days before the perpetual news cycle, because news, like bread, is perishable. Indeed, outdated news is also called stale. Routinization is equally important because the news media must distribute their product more regularly and punctually than most others. As a result, news organizations need predictably available raw materials that can be assembled by a work force in a routine fashion. Efficiency is integral to creating a product cheap enough to serve the audience and advertisers but profitable enough to attract entrepreneurs and investors.[17]

All the basic ingredients that go into news affect how it is produced. To start, journalists must have access to news sources that are credible and can supply them quickly and regularly with events or statements that can be fashioned into news.[18] Stories have to be familiar enough, at least in subject matter, to attract an audience but also novel and thus unfamiliar enough to be deserving of the name news.

The sources that fill the requirements of mass production best are the previously mentioned high-government officials. They have the power and staffs to create newsworthy events (ranging from decisions and activities to ceremonies) or statements (including reports, speeches, and news conferences, among others) regularly and quickly. Their power and authority make them credible sources as well, or more credible to editors and other news executives than sources with less authority and status. Whether they are more credible to more people in the news audience than anyone else remains unknown.

Officials can also schedule many events and statements, estimate on the basis of past experience whether they will become newsworthy stories, and are able to schedule them in time for news deadlines.[19] Consequently, assignment editors can also marshall—and schedule—their limited reportorial resources.[20] When officials create newsworthy events or statements, they also reduce costs for the news media, such as unproductive goose chases for news.[21]

At the same time, the journalistic dependence on high officials has its costs. The source-journalist relationship is symbiotic, for while the sources need the journalists, the journalists also need the sources and therefore cannot afford to alienate them. Journalists may thus be discouraged from pursuing news stories under the official radar. Investigative reporters know how to get information from sources that flourish under this radar, but learn how to do so without seriously displeasing the official sources on whom the news media depend for their everyday raw material.

Needless to say, the mass production analogy is oversimplified, because the news product bears only limited resemblance to its mind-numbing equivalent in factories. Even the most predictable stories from the White House or the local police department are not and cannot be identical to those of the previous day. There is after all no actual mass production and the assembly line is metaphorical.

Furthermore, the world being covered by the news media is always changing and often unpredictable. Consequently, news organizations must be able to break out of the standard routine, including slowing down or stopping the assembly line.

For journalists, the most valued breakouts are "breaking news" that enable them to report important events more or less as they are happening. Such stories give journalists a chance to react to quickly changing situations and on the spur of the moment, to rely on their own observations and use other than routine official sources. Then journalism becomes creative and unusually exciting, making the adrenalin flow, and enabling them to obtain professional fulfillment. Above all, breakouts offer professionals an opportunity to come up with a better story than their competitors or rivals. A small-town reporter who performs unusually well could be offered a big city or national job if the news media are hiring. News organizations have rarely had trouble recruiting war reporters, since wars have consisted of one breaking story after another.[22]

The White House correspondent is at the other extreme, for despite the high status of the position, the journalists occupying it spend most of their time reporting events and statements that must be covered simply because they come from the White House. As a result, the White House is able to formulate a daily message with which to saturate the news media, both to achieve its political aims and to keep out conflicting news stories. At times, the daily message is trumped by breaking news, or by exposés that interrupt the performances that the White House correspondent is expected to report.

Data Reduction: Reactivity, Pegs, and Proxies

One further component of the journalistic mass-production process is the equivalent of what the sociologist Howard S. Becker calls "data reduction," that is, removing overly detailed, irrelevant, and other information that cannot be accommodated in the print or electronic news story. Proper data reduction leaves the journalist responsible for the story with enough information that can be organized and analyzed to produce a story of the right length, and in the writing or tape-editing time available to the journalist.[23] Data reduction occurs at two levels. First, reporters can use only some of the "data" they have collected in their stories, and second, editors or producers must decide how to reduce the large number of stories their staffs collect every day to fit into the limited amount of space or time, or newshole, available in the newspaper, magazine, or news program.[24] The data-reduction practices used by editors or producers affect prior data judgments about newsworthiness, and result in three general practices that are particularly relevant to issues of democracy in the news media: reactivity or passivity, pegs, and proxies.

Reactivity   One of the primary data-reduction practices is limiting the news to reactive or passive reporting, to covering already available stories. Reactive news includes prescheduled events, speeches, press conferences, and the like. Reactivity not only reduces the number of potential stories to be reported but it is efficient; sending reporters out to research or find new ones is time consuming and expensive, and is therefore restricted.

No news medium can afford to depend entirely on passive news, for then only those able to create events would be newsworthy. More important, all the news media would report roughly the same news and could not compete through their story selection and reporting. Pure passivity is impossible anyway; important events require active reporting so that information can be obtained from a number of sources, to report all or at least two sides when conflicts take place, and to iron out conflicting information from various sources. Still, passively obtained news is a mainstay of news production.

Whatever its virtue as a method of data reduction, passive news requires journalists to depend almost entirely on what their sources want to make public, virtually turning them into publicists for these sources and the events and statements scheduled or created by their sources. Completely passive reporting would also disregard news about and from the public figures and citizens who lack the power and resources to schedule predictable, especially predictably newsworthy, events or meet the other requirements of reactivity.

Journalists do not like the reactive aspect of newsgathering, and in fact try to avoid it as much as they can. Breaking news is so desirable because it can only be covered by active reporting, although if journalists have the time and leeway, they will add active reporting of, or even find new stories in, the prescheduled events to which they have been assigned.

The higher the circulations, ratings, and news budgets of the news organizations for which they work, the greater the journalists' ability to undertake active reporting. All other things being equal, print media reporters can be more active than electronic ones, because newspapers have more room for such stories.[25]

Pegs   A second practice of data reduction is the "peg," a metaphoric handle on which usable news can be hung and that helps journalists choose between the numerous alternative stories usually available to them. The primary peg is the date; normally, events and statements taking place that day or week have priority over all others.[26] When stories are equally newsworthy, pegged ones, and those with the earliest peg, usually have priority. Stories with a later peg or no peg at all can be delayed for another day or week, unless they become stale; they can also be canceled if other stories with newer pegs become available.[27]

Because pegged stories are easily distinguisable from unpegged or pegless ones, the peg helps news organizations produce the news as routinely, efficiently, and competitively as possible. At the same time, the peg is yet another device that privileges the prescheduled story, and therefore the public officials and their event-and-statement production machinery. Ever since the 1960s, sophisticated leaders of citizen groups have learned to adapt to the peg and other data-reduction methods, but only the well-organized and reasonably affluent groups can create the necessary infrastructure to produce newsworthy and prescheduled events that can fit easily into the mass-production process. Still, a lot of event creation is needed before the events of a little-known citizen group can compete for newsworthiness with those of a well-known public official.

Proxies The third prominent data-reduction practice is the use of "proxies" that represent other, usually larger or more complicated, institutions and sources. For example, the president, and the other already-mentioned high officials, function as the principal proxies for the government. These proxies enable journalists to cover government on a day-to-day basis and to ignore other officials and agencies until such time as these come up with important or otherwise newsworthy events and statements. The reliance on proxies helps explain the journalists' spotty coverage of government and other institutions, but the chosen proxies also drive the journalists toward many of the same sources as other data-reduction methods.

The major proxy for politics is the presidential election. Now that election campaigns have become permanent, almost any event or statement by an elected official or potential candidate can be reported as part of the official's strategy for the next election. Because almost anything could be considered significant for the next election, journalists have obtained a nearly unlimited reservoir of sources and stories. At times, it appears as if no government decision is ever made if it does not support White House campaign strategy.

Some media critics believe that this journalistic preoccupation with strategy causes public cynicism, contributes to the decline of trust in elected officials, and reduces voter interest in government. The news media are the villains in this scenario, although no reliable evidence exists to suggest that they are responsible for the lack of trust or the public's cynicism.[28] More likely, both stem from people's own observations of politics, particularly at the local level, with the news media perhaps reinforcing their observations. Some data exists to suggest that citizens are more cynical than journalists.[29]

Elections are also proxies for democracy, because they are virtually the only occasion in which citizens play a major in government. As a result, election campaigns, and primary campaigns before them, are often covered in excruciating daily detail, creating the possibility that journalists may not be available to cover other stories, and that such stories might be pushed out of the newshole.[30]

Election campaigns have their own proxy: the horse race that determines who is ahead in the polls from day to day. In recent elections, the horse race has been joined by the money race: stories about who has collected the most hard and soft campaign funds, and from whom. The news media have long been accused of putting the horse race before the issues, but it changes all the time and can thus produce many stories while the issues may remain unchanged from the time they were first introduced into the campaign.[31] Candidates know that journalists cannot repeat their old statements about the issues they are emphasizing, putting pressure on candidates to elaborate on them.

The presidential debates are increasingly viewed as an arena in which the candidates are supposed to discuss only the issues. By then, the candidates are so intellectually punch drunk or risk averse or both that their discussions are actually snatches from their campaign speeches. Partly as a result, those journalists acting as debate monitors are turned into questioners, sometimes forcing the candidates to discuss new issues.[32]

Interestingly enough, the half of eligible citizens who do not vote in presidential elections are rarely covered in pre- and post-election stories.[33] Although pollsters and others reporting the race for the presidency try hard to figure out who is likely to vote, they also pay little or no attention to probable or potential nonvoters. Their numbers are sometimes estimated, but little curiosity appears to exist about their identity or their thoughts about the election and their voting decisions.

True, unless they are habitual nonvoters, they cannot be identified until after the election, but people who have not voted recently and those who are undecided about voting would seem to be appropriate subjects for regular stories.[34] After all, nonvoters play a significant if indirect role in selecting the president and other governmental proxies whom journalists will cover for the next several years.

Journalism's Theory of Democracy and its Shortcomings

The mass-production process is journalism's everyday reality and its major operational problem. Its theory of democracy, as I called it at the start of this book, is its central political ideal.[35] As a theory it is not written down, and as an ideal, it is so widely accepted and thus taken for granted that it is not really discussed. The term democracy itself is only rarely mentioned in the indices of the major journalism texts.

In a way, the theory is also one of the departures from the journalistic operational routine: a normative privilege allowed to journalists to give additional social significance to their work. At the same time, being unwritten, the theory does not really interfere with their routine. Whether or how much it guides that routine is hard to say because journalists must cope with so many demands and pressures just to meet their deadlines.

The roots of the theory can probably be found in the Progressive movement of the early twentieth century, when muckrakers not only began to expose corrupt public officials and political bosses but the magazines that published them also sought "to extend the citizen's power" through direct primaries and other electoral reforms and to bring citizens together through voluntary associations.[36] The Progressives were, among other things, a movement of the educated middle classes who called for the informed citizen and criticized poor and working-class city dwellers for voting for political-machine candidates in exchange for jobs and other favors.[37]

In logical order, the theory consists of four parts: (1) the journalist's role is to inform citizens; (2) citizens are assumed to be informed if they regularly attend to the local, national, and international news journalists supply them; (3) the more informed citizens are, the more likely they are to participate politically, especially in the democratic debate that journalists consider central to participation and democracy; (4) the more that informed citizens participate, the more democratic America is likely to be.[38]

The first part of the theory, concerning journalism's role in informing citizens seems self-evident, but it does not specify what citizens need to be informed about, and what news is and is not essential to advance or maintain democracy. For example, how much of the official top-down news that journalists report so often is really necessary for democracy or would citizens be better served by other news about their elected representatives?

Actually, journalists do not aim merely to inform. Exposés as well as regular stories that report instances of unfairness, injustice, corruption, or malfeasance seek also to warn and even anger people so that they will come together to fight the evils reported in the news. Perhaps journalists want to inform people so they will be persuaded to become activists for clean and competent government.[39] Little is known about the process by which people derive news relevant to their citizenship roles. How do they decide? The question is particularly salient for the many stories about which they cannot do anything, a category that includes most political news.

The second part of the theory assumes that the stories journalists consider newsworthy will turn people into informed citizens. Journalists are not very curious about how the news audience becomes an informed citizenry, but merely supplying them with information does not make them into informed citizens.[40] The people have to participate, for example by wanting and using the information, perhaps by incorporating it into what they already know. Journalists may have to borrow motivational, rhetorical, and educational techniques from teachers so that they can make sure that people become informed.

Many journalists also assume that democracy rests on, and can be maintained by, the political news they report. In effect, the theory asks little of journalists other than what they already do on the job, although they justify their work by an ostensibly citizen-based formula: "the public's need to know."[41] How journalists decide what people need, or how people themselves decide what they need, has not received sufficient consideration.

Furthermore, journalists themselves are automatically assumed to be capable of informing citizens, and thus to be informed themselves. Although they are surely better informed than their audience, most are generalists who sometimes know little about the subjects of their stories before they report them, and who do not always get enough time to educate themselves properly. Beat reporters, who are often experts, are the exceptions. Those who cover the main domestic and foreign beats are highly informed about the beats they cover and have covered in the past.

In addition, news is not merely information. Journalists also speculate when information is lacking; they assign motives to the political actors on whom they report, and they pass on information, as well as misinformation, publicity, and propaganda fed to them by their sources.[42] Their stories include the myths, stereotypes, and biases that are prevalent in their social circles and in the country's newsrooms.

The final product must survive the data-reduction and other practices of the mass-production process; it is chosen to fit the time and space available as well as the commercial and other requirements that journalists must consider. The informational needs of the citizenry can only be a secondary consideration.

The third part of the theory argues that once citizens are informed, they will feel compelled to participate politically. But that is not often the case. Although audience studies indicate that informed people are more likely to participate politically than others, their participation, whether in voting or organizational activity results from their higher levels of income and education.

Whatever the virtues of a good education, however, many people become politically active without being informed by journalistic (or other) standards. If people want to make demands on their representatives, to protest, or to protect their interests and values, they do not let inadequate information, or for that matter, the facts get in the way of what they do. They may even restrict their news intake to information supporting their positions, and at times, may create falsehoods or use rumors to justify these positions. Indeed, misinformation may be more effective than information for creating the anger that often motivates the most intense participation.

For better or worse, no informational threshold exists for citizenship. Nor can such a requirement exist without drastic revisions in our democratic concepts and rules of citizenship. Questions about whether, when, and how uninformed or misinformed citizens can harm democracy deserve to be asked, but not without also considering whether such citizens may disagree with the political preferences and policies of the informed.[43]

Yet other questions can be raised about the unilateral conception of information that underlies journalism. Information that is relevant to one person may be irrelevant to another, and people at different levels of the social hierarchy, age groups, and other background variations are likely to need different information. Investors in stocks and bonds do not need information about welfare regulations, which is why such information does not appear in newspaper business pages.

More important, however, the theory's conception of participation, as of the citizenry, is unrealistic. As a diverse people with a variety of values and interests, citizens participate accordingly. Consequently, citizen participation is a process full of conflicts, often the same conflicts that are central to the rest of the political enterprise. Participation is democratic, but by itself does nothing to solve the problems of the polity or the society.

The third part of the theory also proposes that one important form of citizen participation is involvement in citizen debates and discussions. Journalists, amongst others, seem to believe that "conversation" contributes to democracy. But they do not indicate how the conversing translates into or influences the issues and other considerations that go into the political decision-making by elected officials.[44] No one has even charted the processes by which the conclusions of citizen political conversation can reach the public officials for whom they are intended.

To be sure, politics cannot proceed without talk, and congressional representatives often go back to their districts on weekends to talk with some of their constituents. Undoubtedly, some of the representatives also come to discuss, particularly when they need to sound out constituents to make their voting decisions. But more often they rush from gathering to gathering to be seen, and to field requests from constituents. All this is a proper part of representative democracy, but it is not the kind of discussion the journalists' theory has in mind.

Elected representatives also debate each other on the floor of Congress, although these debates are sometimes performed set pieces to impress constituents while the more important arguments that precede the writing and passing of legislation take place in congressional committee meetings. But at times the floor debates are important. Journalists do not often cover debates, although they see the general discourse between politicians and, more important, arguments over the shape of legislation as a kind of debate they report on consistently. Usually, these debates are two-sided, reflecting the fact that they take place between the two major political parties.

The exchanges that are held on television shortly before elections are called debates, but the candidates in fact try to minimize debating, largely for fear of making unrehearsed statements or mistakes that could hurt them at the polls. Citizens are sometimes allowed to ask questions, but they cannot interact spontaneously with the candidates. Mostly, citizens are spectators.

Perhaps journalists consider citizen dialogue the spontaneous discussions that people carry on over actual or imagined picket fences, at water coolers, on bar stools, coffeeshop chairs, and now in internet chatrooms.[45] Some may also be thinking of feature stories reporting debates among citizens (often experts) set up by newspapers and magazines, or debates among journalists that take place on editorial and op ed pages and TV talk shows.[46] Even the news itself is sometimes seen as an example of the democratic debate.

Debates and discussions may inform citizens, but unless they lead to or affect citizen participation and their conclusions are communicated to elected officials, they cannot make the direct contribution to democracy suggested by the journalistic theory. They are not exempt, either, from ending up as bitter arguments over values and interests.

This is not meant to denigrate political discussions or debates and their potential to motivate political learning or activity, but rather to suggest that they do not automatically produce politically relevant solutions. Nor can they be guaranteed to contribute to democracy, for debates among participants of unequal power do not resolve power differences. That the participants have different opinions or come from contrasting interest or ideological groups and meet to thrash out their differences will surely enrich them. But journalistic faith in the powers of debate notwithstanding, the exchange alone cannot overcome differences or achieve compromises.

However admirable journalistic faith may be, it masks the difficulty many citizens have communicating with others who hold conflicting views on matters both feel strongly about. People who are not experienced with or trained in politics often have trouble compromising. Journalists who cover public meetings often witness shouting matches between disagreeing citizens. Unfortunately, the ideal built into journalistic theorizing frequently clashes with political realities or observed human behavior.

The fourth part of the theory, that more participation means a more democratic America is wishful thinking, for neither an informed citizenry nor political activity, whether by citizens or officials, necessarily produce democracy.

Informed citizens have been known to overthrow dictatorships but they have also supported them. Moreover, democracy seems to require a properly functioning economy, a reasonably egalitarian society, secure working and middle classes, and a variety of other prerequisites in addition to those stated in the U.S. Constitution.

Even in an otherwise democratic society, active citizens rarely have the power to stand up against undemocratic political organizations, especially when the latter have the power to control the strategic levers of politics and government. Current events suggest how difficult it is for such citizens to break up today's close ties between lobbyists, campaign funders, and elected officials. Social movements as well as drastic electoral shifts can at times neutralize or eliminate undemocratic political groups and cut the ties that connect the powerful, but these kinds of political participation require large numbers of organized and mobilized citizens.

Even so, the theory's most serious shortcoming for journalists may be its proposition that the information they supply to the public automatically enhances democracy. This proposition assumes that information, like knowledge, is power, which sometimes encourages journalists to claim to "empower" the news audience. In reality, however, the reverse is true: power creates knowledge. In political institutions as in most others, citizens must obtain power—and access to the above-mentioned strategic levers—before they can obtain the right information, i.e., the facts and data bases that enable them to exercise and maintain power.

Citizens also have to be in the right places to discover what information is most relevant for participation in governmental decision making, and from what sources it can be obtained. Even then, they still need enough influence, and the right political contacts, to actually obtain it. Powerful political organizations are good at depriving the citizenry—as well as journalists—of information that might reduce their own power. Information that enables people to obtain or sustain power bears little resemblance to journalist-disseminated news, so the news that journalists supply to the news audience cannot increase their political power.

Like the news, information is always plentiful, but when it is politically irrelevant, people who inform themselves in order to exercise their democratic rights may simply wind up with a bad case of information overload. For example, although domestic political priorities often influence foreign policy, ordinary citizens rarely have much direct say about American foreign policy. However, they had no more say when the news media reported a greater amount of foreign news.

The blindness of the journalistic theory of democracy to the existence of power, including economic power, also hampers journalistic understanding of the political process. Journalists are skilled reporters of the ever-increasing economic and political influence of well-organized interest groups, but the coverage has not yet sufficiently penetrated journalistic thinking about the democratic ideal. In fact, busy and often overworked journalists barely think about democracy, since it is rarely relevant to story selection and other editorial decision making. Perhaps the theory serves as a substitute for thinking about democracy.

Journalism itself is hurt by the theory's various shortcomings. Journalists fail to see its self-serving aspects, for example, that the news they choose on commercial grounds is sufficient to create informed citizens. Thus, they do not understand sufficiently how much the way they view democracy satisfies their own interests. Its superficiality and inaccuracies can get in their way when they analyze the politics they cover in everyday practice, and these shortcomings may also prevent them from seeing the larger forces that drive politics. The idealism built into the journalistic theory may even hide their inability to do much on behalf of democracy.

Downplaying the Economy

A final shortcoming of the journalists' democratic theory is its narrowness, for it is almost completely limited to politics and pays little attention to the other parts of society that affect the country's democracy.[47] The most important part is the economy, and its impact on American democracy and on the polity in general is missing from the theory.

The economy is also underplayed in the news media themselves. Although a dramatic increase in reporting economic news has taken place in recent years among the elite national newspapers, it is still sparse in the other news media. Television news has never been able to figure out how to reconcile its hunger for moving pictures with the fact that much of the available economic news is about numbers. Even in the print media, most economic news is really business news intended to inform investors and much of the rest appears when firms and other economic institutions run afoul of government regulations.

Altogether, the news media pay attention to four kinds of domestic economic news stories. First, corporate and union funding of election campaigns and of their lobbying of the government afterwards are covered extensively. However, the typical story is about the size of the contributions. Detailed reporting of the political influence of the contributors and lobbyists is rare. Journalists raise the suspicion that campaign funds buy "access," and if post-election legislation that benefits the contributors is passed, the stories assume that the contributions are the cause of the legislation.

Whether and when this assumption is justified deserves more legwork than it receives, and few stories are written about the actual economic or political consequences of the legislation for the funders, elected officials, and the country.[48] Estimates of the costs of contributor access for citizens are reported only occasionally. Even the kinds of industries and firms that contribute routinely and undramatically and the reasons they contribute do not seem to be particularly newsworthy, and journalists almost never look into the firms and industries that do not contribute to election campaigns or hire well-known Washington lobbyists. The news media report the frequent "pork-barrel" bills that elected officials use to demonstrate their utility to their constituents, but journalists do not say much about which constituents, including campaign contributors, benefit from the pork-barrel projects.

The impact of other aspects of the economy on democracy also gets little play. Journalists report only irregularly, and then mostly in passing, on how the wealth and income of citizens affect whether or how they vote, which politicians they support, and what issues interest them.[49] Stories about how people react politically when unemployment strikes, and what roles, if any, the unemployed play in politics are also unusual. The politics of soccer moms have received more play than that of assembly-line or lawyer moms, not to mention the poor moms who try to raise children with minimum-wage jobs.

Second, journalists have always reported when businesses get into legal trouble with, or are taken to court by, government agencies, one reason why the news media have supplied so much coverage of the disintegration of Enron. Firms in trouble with government is, however, a standard government story category that applies to all well-known violators of the law. Enron's widespread campaign contributions, extensive lobbying, and connections to high officials in the Bush Administration also made it a political story.

The economic consequences of the company's collapse for its executives and its ordinary employees combined law violation with human interest. Enron's generosity to Texas cultural and other institutions spread the story into yet other sections of the news media. Enron also provided raw material for stories about the immense salaries and stock bonuses paid to corporate executives. This is one of the few instances in which American economic inequality appears in the news. Although most of the stories report the incomes of executives who, like Enron's and Tyco's, have gotten into trouble with the government, other CEOs who have ended up with higher incomes while their companies were losing money have also become newsworthy.

Even so, these exposés have not yet encouraged journalists to look critically into related subjects, for example, corporate profits. In fact, high profits are reported positively on business pages when corporations issue their annual reports, but abnormally high profits, unusual windfalls and the like are not now newsworthy. Of course, journalists do not report firms that earn unreasonable profits, but then they also do not identify the firms that pay unreasonably low wages. Neither they nor members of other mainstream institutions normally think in terms of unreasonable profits or wages, although journalists report when firms are caught by the government paying illegally low wages.[50]

Third, the news media report rates of unemployment, inflation, poverty, and the rise and fall in consumer purchases, gross national product, and other economic indicators, but they usually do little more than reprint monthly and other periodic government reports. Often they just rewrite the government's news releases. Perhaps journalists should not be expected to plow through the statistics made available with the news releases, but in relying on news releases, they unwittingly accept the government's indicators, and the ways these are measured. In this country as elsewhere, these tend to understate negative statistics, for example, about the actual rates of poverty and unemployment.[51]

In recent years, the news media have, however, expanded their coverage of economic indicators. For example, many newspapers now keep track of the total number of layoffs across the country and layoff estimates are often mentioned when two big corporations merge. Moreover, a larger number of stories about the economy appear with every turn in the business cycle. Globalization has helped to increase the flow, but mostly because news about tariff policies and the actions of the International Monetary Fund and the World Bank are governmental stories. How multinationals operate on a day-to-day basis, and how they affect democracy and politics in the United States are not often reported, however.

Generally speaking, the news media pay more attention to "management" than to "labor."[52] News about employees is more often about professionals than about white-collar workers or technicians, and the nearly half of the population that still describes itself as working class receives even shorter shrift. For example, during the last quarter century or so, Silicon Valley, the computer industry, and the dramatic rise and fall of the dot coms have been reported extensively, but little coverage has appeared about the wages and working conditions of the men and women, a goodly number of them immigrants or poorly paid members of American racial minorities, who manufacture the hardware and software that make the digital economy possible.[53]

Now that unions enroll only about 10 percent of American workers and many are too weak to strike, workplace dissatisfaction is no longer a newsworthy story.[54] In fact, business journalists often write about workers as a production factor called "labor" that is relevant mainly in estimating costs of production rather than as members of the firms for which they work.

The problems of the economy in which most people spend most of their waking time are rarely story material. Threats to job security, deficiencies in job safety and other working conditions, various kinds of inequalities between the several strata in the workplace pecking order, and all the other workplace and economic concerns of the employed part of the news audience are usually reported only when laws are broken and government intervenes. In effect, they are virtually never reported.[55]

Unemployment fell off the news pages and TV news programs during the economic boom of the late 1990s when unskilled workers dominated the lists of the jobless. Even during the period when downsizing was a popular buzzword, it received only a small number of mentions in the news media.[56]

The rise in employment that followed the downsizing period was first mainly covered as a threat to the low rate of inflation.[57] Whenever new increases in employment were reported, the Federal Reserve Bank and other government agencies began to express their concern about inflation—and the journalists went right along. The journalists gave no sign of noticing that what their sources called inflation spelled higher wages for the employed, including themselves. Indeed, their preoccupation with inflation persuaded economic journalist John Cassidy to write that "when a working stiff demands a pay raise, it causes inflation and threatens the nation's prosperity; when a CEO gets a raise ten thousand times as large, it rewards enterprise and assures all our futures."[58]

The criteria of newsworthiness that give short shrift to ordinary workers and downplay unemployment are not new. Even during the Great Depression, when such subjects, and the difficulties of the unemployed or those working "short weeks" might have been expected to be the dominant news story, the news media marched to another drummer. Although studies of how the journalists covered the Depression are virtually nonexistent, the news pages appear to have stayed with news about government and politics, focusing mainly on the conflicts between government and employers.[59] Only spot coverage of changes in employment, unemployment, and related statistics was provided.

One reason for the omission was overtly political. Newspaper publishers discouraged their own reporters from regular stories about the country's joblessness, fearing it would cause a further decline in business confidence and the capitalist system.[60] Columnists were apparently no more eager to discuss the country's economic problems; instead, they wrote about what they viewed as the dangers of economic planning.[61]

The fourth type of story about the economy is also the most frequently covered: a category called "business," a set of activities that almost seem independent of the economy, and are therefore covered by business sections, not only in newspapers but also news magazines, television news, and on cable's business channels. As a section, "business" is not very different from "arts," "travel," "style," "sports," and other sections devoted to consumer industries.[62]

The similarity is not coincidental, for the business section is itself filled largely with stories about the selling and buying of stocks, bonds, and mutual funds and of the firms that do the selling and buying. Much of the rest of the economic news is about events and statements that affect, or could affect, stock prices. For example, much of the coverage of the decline and fall of Enron reported on those aspects that had a major impact on the company stock's continuing loss of value. Business stories are thus mainly about the consumer industry around investments.[63]

Perhaps the best indicator of the primacy of business is that the main news media proxy for the economy, which is reported daily in newspapers and updated constantly on the internet, radio, and cable television, is the Dow Jones Index. Despite its name, it is actually the daily price list for a carefully selected, but not always representative, sample of 30 of the several thousand stocks traded on the major stock exchanges. In addition, most newspapers publish pages of daily stock prices. No index exists for daily fluctuations in the price of bread, milk, ground meat, and other basic dietary staples, however. No one publishes a section reporting store prices of the major necessities and luxuries—or of the wages and salaries being paid in major occupational categories.

Business sections already existed in newspapers when their audience was a small set of professional investors, speculators, and the very rich and their financial advisers. In the last quarter century, the business section has expanded to serve the increasing proportion of the news audience that invests its savings mostly in mutual funds. The daily listing of mutual funds is now part of the stock pages in a number of newspapers. The business section's increased attention to mutual funds and small stock purchases has attracted new advertisers, expanded the section newshole, and considerably enlarged the section staff. The number of business journalists has risen from 4,800 in 1988 to over 12,000 in 1999.[64]

The increase in business news has undoubtedly helped pay for the reporters who write about the general economy and the institutions and activities that have nothing to do with stocks and stock prices. The number of such journalists is rising but they remain a small minority of the business journalists. Still, no one seems to be aware of the institutional bias inherent in relegating the economy to a subsection of business.

Why so little economic news? For one thing, businesses, unions, and other nongovernmental economic players are under no obligation to supply news to journalists, nor do they often need to do so. Although firms send publicity releases to the news media about their new appointments and routine matters like annual shareholder meetings, businesses can communicate their news through purchased publicity or advertisements that also allow them to communicate their version of reality. Furthermore, journalists who write about the economy usually obtain information from economists employed by banks or investment firms, who are more likely to offer business versions than labor economists or academic ones.

In addition, the business community is protected by privacy rules that can bar journalists and prevent them from gathering news that could hurt business firms. Even so, the news media occasionally undertake investigative reporting in business firms, and do so despite a threatened or actual loss of advertising. News firms can generally tolerate such losses, but they turn nervous when businesses bring suit after exposés about them appear.

Government officials lack these protections and are expected to make themselves available to journalists. They also bear the brunt of journalistic exposés. However, being unable to buy advertising to report what they are doing, they need the journalists to inform the citizenry and to publicize their activities.

Intentionally or not, government thus ensures that the news media pay maximal attention to it. Meanwhile, business makes equally sure that the news media keep regular tabs on government, but not on business.

The news media also downplay economic news because it does not fit into the news media mass-production process. Business people, union officers, and economists are not the kinds of news sources who can regularly create newsworthy events. Thus, the speed, efficiency, and routinization of government-produced news cannot be duplicated. A convenient handful of proxies is also lacking; the economy has no White House, elections, or campaign races. The Dow Jones index is a reliable proxy because it appears daily; the stock market is perceived to be a national institution; and the Index can therefore represent the national economy. Although it is a speedily, efficiently, and routinely reported news source, it is not a very colorful one, lacking the drama of politics or the game of elections.

Journalistic tradition supports downplaying the economy, among other reasons because many newspapers began as subsidiaries of political parties.[65] The tradition is supported further by mainstream American ideology in which the economy is viewed as separate from the political system. Thus, the political consequences of what happens in the economy are newsworthy only when they become visible, for example when corporate executives become major campaign contributors, or bad economic times cause control of Congress to shift from one political party to the other. At other times, the news media do not appear to see that the state of the economy is a 24/7 ingredient of the political process, if not always the dominating one.[66]

Journalists themselves trace the scarcity of economic reporting to their being generalists, untrained in economics and often fearful of statistical analysis and even numbers. They also believe the news audience to be uninterested in most economic news. They are probably correct, for the economy is not easily turned into attention-getting stories, and making it comprehensible to an audience largely uneducated in economics is difficult. That audience might pay more attention if economic news dealt with corporate conflicts as it does with conflicts among elected officials, or if the national economy were covered as and in stories about the local economies where the newspaper audience actually earns its living. Indeed, that audience might even be more interested in the national economy if journalists covered it more often from the perspective of employees and consumers. Perhaps economic journalists could make economic news more appealing by borrowing some leads from the folk economics with which people make sense of their personal experiences in the economy.

Problems and Democratic Implications

Although many of the problems of the news media and journalists discussed in this chapter apply to everyday routine newsgathering and reporting, I have considered these problems largely as obstacles to the journalists' contribution to democracy. If journalists had more of an opportunity to pursue the profession's democratic ideal, they would have to consider how to reorganize the journalistic assembly line so as to reduce the emphasis on top-down news and the publicizing of the powerful. They would also have to discard the data-reduction methods they now use—or find new ones—that might make citizens more newsworthy. But the journalists would first have to make news firms take responsibility for the economic and logistic costs that accompany these changes.

Until this can happen, journalists have enough to do to rethink their democratic ideal, relate it more closely to the democratic realities they report every day, and figure out how to proceed from reality to the ideal. At the same time, they need to broaden the ideal and make all the components of American society that impinge on democracy as newsworthy as politics.

Some of the problems discussed in this chapter will turn up again in Chapter 5, when I consider what can be done to move journalistic practice toward the democratic ideal. Before then, however, I need to look at the effects the news and the news media have on the news audience and the country. When journalists can make an impact on people's behavior and attitudes, or on the actions of organizations and institutions, the news can also make a difference in government and politics. However, when effects are absent or limited, so is the journalists' ability to help move the country closer to the democratic ideal.

CHAPTER 4

The Problem of News Effects

When people read, view, or listen to the news, they may remember some of the stories and forget some—or all of them. However, some news stories impress themselves on people's minds and emotions strongly enough that they have an effect on their opinions or behavior. For news stories to have such an effect, they must be relevant to people's lives. The coverage of the events of 9/11 are in this category. That news affected people's opinions about American domestic and foreign policies, for example, as well as their behavior.

If news has no impact, it is ephemeral; only when it has effects can the news help to change society.[1] Consequently, even if journalism's methods and practices were more focused on the profession's democratic ideal, the resulting changes in the news would still need to affect the audience before journalists could aid any movement toward a citizens' democracy.

Actually, the news alone is not likely to have much effect of any kind, for it is largely the people, statements, events, and topics about which the news reports that have effects. To put it another way, most news effects are indirect, for the news media function mainly as messengers for the people and events that make news.

Messengers are crucial, for without them, people could not obtain news beyond their own personal contacts and social circles. Even so, journalists cannot function as messengers unless the recipients want and need them; otherwise, their messages remain unattended. This is the fate of much political news, for government's impact on people's lives is limited, and often indirect as well.

I use "limited" deliberately, for ever since media research began almost a century ago, researchers have argued over two theories. One theory insists that the mass media have limited or minor effects; the other states that its effects are unlimited. The latter theory is sometimes called the hypodermic theory, because the media are seen as a stimulus that, like a hypodermic, have a regular and unvarying response. Many people in the general public believe in the hypodermic theory, that television violence leads to real-life violence, for example, and that erotica results in increased sexual activity and even rape.

The popular belief in the hypodermic theory is backed up by the fact that we are surrounded by a variety of mass media and that they should thus have some impact on us. In fact, many people swear that the media is a potent force capable of changing American life, especially in disagreeable ways.

"The media" is probably best thought of as a modern equivalent for "evil spirits," for the actual mass media are large in number and transmit an equally large and often contradictory variety of messages. The stimuli coming from the actual media can neither produce a single and homogeneous audience nor create a single effect on people.

In fact, the mass media, especially those supplying popular entertainment, have also responded to stimuli from the audience and have been affected by changes in that audience. For example, the sharp rise in premarital sex and adolescent sexual activity began long before the mass media dared to include them openly in their programming, and even now nudity and sexual acts remain virtually as taboo in commercial television as in the 1960s.[2] Conversely, in Europe, erotic and even pornographic television have been available for at least a generation, but sexual activity still begins somewhat later than it does in America.

Moreover, if American television violence had the effects the hypodermic theory predicts, Americans would have been killing each other in humongous numbers ever since television became a mass medium. The theory of limited effects offers a better explanation than the hypodermic one.[3]

In the news media, effects research is almost totally nonexistent, but the most that can normally be expected from the news media are limited effects, and even these are likely to be unpredictable. For example, a 1987 NBC television story about the Ethiopian famine resulted in a flood of donations, while other stories of overseas famines and disasters, such as in the Sudan or in Rwanda and Burundi, produced no such reaction from the American news audience.[4]

Media effects are also limited because people tend to filter the news by selective perception, paying attention mainly to stories they consider useful, relevant, or gripping.[5] Selective perception helps ensure that except on special occasions, people pay more attention to stories that accord with the values and predispositions they bring to the media. Ever since political advertising was introduced on television, voters with parties affiliations and sympathies have watched the ads of their parties more often than the ads of opposing parties. Partly because of the power of selective perception, the news media are thought to reinforce, strengthen, and even to legitimate, existing attitudes and behaviors rather than to change them.[6]

How the News Affects People

Because so little research has been done on the effects of the news media, this chapter is largely speculative, consisting mainly of hypotheses about such effects.[7] For brevity's sake, I state my hypotheses as if effects were uniform across the news media, but print and electronic news media sometimes have different effects, especially in the short term.

Furthermore, the hypotheses that follow actually describe potential effects, effects that may or may not be realized.[8] People who earn their living with words, pictures, and other symbols, including journalists, sociologists, media critics, and the like, pay close attention to the news and other media. Most people in the news audience pay far less attention to the news and misunderstand some of it as well. Consequently, many of the potential effects of the news media never occur.

The most definitive findings about news media effects have come from laboratory research.[9] However, laboratory studies systematically overestimate the effects of the news, because people participating in the experiments concentrate far more on the news in the laboratory than they do at home.[10]

Laboratory studies support one finding that has been reported outside the laboratory: news media effects are generally superficial and short term, so much so that people have difficulty remembering what news stories they saw or read only hours earlier.[11] Their recall is diminished by the fact that both on television and the internet, old news stories are constantly replaced by new ones.

In the list that follows, I begin with effects mainly on people and follow with effects on organizations, institutions, and the country.

The Social Continuity Effect   The news media's basic, though rarely acknowledged, effect may be its demonstration of social continuity. In some respects, the news is like the sun; its daily appearance as scheduled is a sign that social life will go on as before. This effect is probably unconscious, but the news appears regularly every day, filled largely with routine stories, from the president's activities to the Dow Jones Index. Whatever else they communicate, the news media and the news enable people to take for granted that the social order continues to exist.

This role becomes particularly important when the news is about disaster and disorder, as journalists can be counted on to begin to report recovery efforts and the move back toward order as quickly as possible. As in the case of the assassination of John F. Kennedy or the destruction of New York's World Trade Center, the news media made sure to show, and repeatedly so, that the social order and the structure of authority had not been impaired. Not long after President Kennedy's death had been announced, television journalists began to speculate on how and when Vice President Lyndon B. Johnson would be sworn in.

The continuity effect can be illustrated further with a thought experiment that outlines what might happen if the news media closed down.[12] Without the news media, everyday routines would soon be interrupted. The government could continue to function for a while using its interoffice media, but it would be impaired and ultimately paralyzed when it needed to reach people and institutions and was unable to do so.

Some Americans might be happy without political news, but no government can long continue to govern without communicating with the citizenry. Even if people ignore much of the communication, political news is a sign that the government is still governing. This is particularly necessary in a crisis, otherwise questions about the country's stability would quickly arise all over the world.[13]

Americans might also be concerned about possible governmental misbehavior in the absence of political news. Without journalists to watch and report, elected officials might do more and greater favors for the funders of their election campaigns and government bureaucrats might decide not to show up for work.[14] Interest groups and their representatives would seek government help they would not dare request if journalists were around to publicize their activities. Public officials might even make controversial decisions, including badly needed but politically risky ones they would be less likely to make if they were reported in the news.[15]

Without the news media, the continuity of democracy itself could be questioned. Elections would be difficult or impossible to conduct because prospective voters would not know who was running and on what issues. Campaign commercials would probably be even less credible than they are now because they would not be surrounded by the journalists' news stories about the campaign.

Journalists even shore up the rules of everyday public life. Although crime news tells people that crime is still taking place, the absence of such news might stimulate feverish imaginations that crime will rise because the criminals need not fear being reported. Suspicions about a rise in crime also heighten the fear of crime. The absence of news practically guarantees the arrival of rumors to supply information when people need it.

The Informing Effect Journalists obviously aim to inform their audience, but equally obviously, the people in the audience choose when they want to inform themselves, and on what topics. Journalists usually report important news whether they think the audience is interested or not, believing that the importance of a story may encourage audience interest.

No one really knows on what subjects the various sectors of the news audience actually inform themselves or let themselves be informed.[16] On political knowledge, the existing studies are contradictory, some suggesting that large numbers of people know little about basic political facts, others indicating that people know enough about major political issues to develop attitudes about them. The ability of poll respondents to answer many of the questions they are asked appears to support that finding.[17]

Presumably, people acquaint themselves most eagerly with information they need for their everyday lives, or can use for emergencies and other crises.[18] More likely, they "keep up" in some general way with those parts of the external environment they do not monitor personally, checking out particular dangers and perhaps opportunities that are reported by the journalists in it. Undoubtedly, people occasionally wander off their principal areas of interest, perhaps attracted by a headline or by accident, they end up exploring a political or other story they would normally ignore. The possible existence of such accidental effects justifies journalists to present whatever news they think the public "needs to know."[19]

Some indirect light on what people inform themselves about is shed by a Pew Center study that began in 1986 and asks respondents every month if they followed a number of specific news stories "very closely, fairly closely, not too closely or not at all closely."[20] The major inference to be drawn from this study is that most people do not follow most news very closely.[21]

Judging by the stories the largest number of poll respondents have said they followed very closely, the top subjects between 1986 and 2001 were wars in which Americans were involved, and disasters, natural and human-made.[22] The top story during that time was the 1986 explosion of the space shuttle *Challenger* that killed six astronauts as the audience watched the blastoff.[23] It was followed "very

closely" by 80 percent of the respondents. The second and third most closely followed stories were the 9/11 tragedies and the subsequent anthrax scare, followed
very closely by 74 and 78 percent, respectively.[24] The differences between the two
percentages are small, but it appears that the anthrax scare, which was national,
hit slightly closer to home than the tragedies on the East Coast.

Political and economic stories that relate to personal concerns, such as federal healthcare proposals, economic downturns and recessions, as well as
gasoline price increases, are next on the list. With some exceptions, events
that upset or concern people from coast to coast are followed very closely most
often.

Of course, the news media do not have a monopoly on informing people.
News also trickles down at the dinner table and the water cooler, and it is entirely possible that the news stories people follow very closely most often are
those reported to them by friends and family members, who have selected
these stories from those they picked up in the news media.[25] Circulation and
rating figures do not reveal whether this news audience is more willing to be
informed by informal rather than professional journalists.[26]

A number of people, especially among the young, apparently obtain some
of their news from the music they listen to, television entertainment programs
that use topics of the day for story material, and the monologues of Jay Leno,
David Letterman, and their peers on "Comedy Central" and elsewhere. They
report the incidents of the adult world with a satirical, ironic, or cynical frame,
which may be treated as news by viewers with similar frames, especially those
with disdain for "straight" news.[27]

Legitimation and Control Effects   Comedians make fun of, and in the process question, the legitimacy of the people they skewer; journalists, on the
other hand, treat the sources and institutions on which they report respect-
fully and earnestly, thus awarding them the legitimation that comes with being
newsworthy. The fact that so much of the news is reported by authoritative
figures from authoritative sources helps to legitimate the less well-known subjects and people that journalists cover.[28] When a local story appears in the national news, the figures in it obtain the legitimacy that goes with being in the
national spotlight, particularly in a country with as much regional, cultural,
and other diversity as America.

The news media may also legitimate information that the news audience
has already learned from personal experience or from family and friends.[29]
News about a rise in inflation people have already noticed in their own shop-

ping not only adds to the credibility of the news but validates the public's experience as well.[30]

Legitimation also implies control. When the news media indulged in the flag waving and hyperpatriotism after 9/11 that they display at the start of every war, they support the government's ability to control opposition to the war.[31] On a subtler level, the news media exert control by creating a mainstream snapshot of the country that excludes or downgrades competing snapshots. During elections, the excluded snapshots are those of minority party candidates, so unwittingly, the news media help to control the electoral field for the major party candidates.[32] Often, the exclusion results from the limited size of the newshole, but the journalists' dependence on authoritative sources also drives them toward the mainstream.

Journalists do not mind displeasing the government, advertisers, or any critic with an agenda based on self-interest, for it demonstrates the correctness of their reporting, at least to themselves. Advertisers are thought to be major content controllers, but most cannot afford the loss of goodwill that might follow their attempts at news censorship. They may withdraw advertising from media that report bad news about them, except that many need the exposure for their ads as badly as the news media need the advertising.[33] Whether the big advertisers and the giant conglomerates behind them can afford to censor the news firms they own and can afford the loss of goodwill that results remains to be seen. Sometimes, a surprisingly small number of unhappy customers can cause economic and other troubles even for giants.

Despite the belief that the news media exert a good deal of control over audience behavior, more often the news audience controls the media. Because parents want to shield their children from being scared by the news, American war casualties, particularly bloodied ones, are virtually never shown. For similar reasons, profanity and related subjects do not appear in "family newspapers" or on television news programs shown around dinner time. The control effects of the news audience were particularly visible after 9/11. Although the news media were accused of initiating the national flag waving after the tragedy, they were actually following the lead of vocal patriots in their audience, who criticized journalists who took too neutral a stance toward the war against terrorism or tried to explain why the terrorists hated America. The media's patriotism may in turn have helped silence opposition against popular patriotism, thus unintentionally helping the government reduce disagreement with its policies.

Effects on Opinions   The most important question about news media effects is their impact on people's opinions and actions, and the answer would help determine what the news media could do for the citizens' role in democracy. However, people's opinions are influenced by so many factors that isolating news media effects is extremely difficult.

Moreover, journalists are as American as their audiences, and often share their opinions. When possible, and within limits, they also try to report news on subjects they believe will interest their audience. The news audience offered clear enough evidence of its low level of interest in foreign news to enable news firms to reduce the amount of foreign news. In this and other ways, the audience also has an effect on, and sets the agenda for, the journalists.[34]

Furthermore, most of the time, most of the news audience pays too little attention to the news for it to have much effect on them. Elected officials can make laws that reduce the incomes or restrict the freedoms of the voters, but voters take a long time to notice such acts and even then may not react. People's unwillingness to pay attention to the news when their direct and high-priority interests are being threatened is infuriating to people who are actively fighting these threats but it has been going on for a long time and no one has yet discovered a remedy.

Memorable events may have an impact on people's opinions. A particularly brutal crime raises the proportion of the public that favor the death penalty; freeing an innocent person who has been awaiting execution may increase the proportion opposing the death penalty. The figures usually do not go up or down significantly, but if pollsters ask general questions when a specific event relevant to such questions is on people's minds, their answers are apt to be influenced by it.[35]

If journalists express overt opinions, which is rare, or use words or tones to indicate their covert opinions, they tend to express mainstream or centrist views. Journalists may indicate that they are against inflation and unemployment or that they oppose the overthrow of democratic foreign governments, but because these are also publicly accepted values, they likely reflect the opinions of most of their audience.

Journalistic centrism notwithstanding, the news media are only rarely able to affect more deeply or permanently held opinions and the values underlying them. Despite the innumerable news stories to which people are exposed, they continue to express remarkably stable opinions on many long-term economic and political issues; they support moderately progressive taxation, expansion of medical services and other components of the welfare state, and provision of jobs when the economy falters and the like. Indeed, on general questions, pluralities or majorities of poll respondents continue to sound like loyal liberals, thus confusing observers when the country's politics turn sharply to the right. However, in conservative times, poll respondents tend to answer more conservatively on topical issues of the moment, and their votes do not necessarily follow their responses to poll questions.

If and when the news media have an informational monopoly, they can affect opinions, but usually about a story about which people in the news audience care little and are not likely to get opinions from elsewhere. If people have opinions about a coup d'etat in a small Asian republic, these have probably been affected by the news media.[36]

By the late 1960s, a large number of people decided that the Vietnam war was unwinnable even while the news continued to report the Pentagon's version of the war. Most likely, these people interpreted the evidence they obtained from the news differently than the journalists' sources intended.

Effects on Activities   The news media's effects on how people act are similar to their effects on opinions. People are bombarded with suggestions about how they should act by everyone from family members to advertisers. The news media are a minor player in this bombardment, but the news neither tells people how to act nor does it report much news on which they could act. News from the White House does not require people to do anything, and the State Department does not consult the news audience about foreign policy.

News stories may occasionally change audience votes or at times, persuade people to participate more actively when journalists dig up an attention-getting story that would otherwise go unknown. Exposés that send villains to jail can anger enough people to drive incumbent politicians out of office. The farther the subject of the exposé is from audience concerns, however the less likely it is to bring about change. "Harvest of Shame," a classic 1950s television documentary about the exploitation and mistreatment of migrant farm workers in the Florida orange groves, did not reduce the mistreatment of the workers, nor did subsequent documentaries on the same subject.[37]

Probably the most drastic behavioral effect of the mass media is imitation, when news stories about murders, suicides, and now, school shootings, are followed by other such acts. Instances of imitation are very rare, and closer examination usually reveals that other factors are considerably more important and that the imitations differ substantially from the acts depicted in the news.[38] Sometimes, imitations turn out to be widespread occurrences that local journalists did not notice or report until a national story made them newsworthy. The most famous example is the 1964 story of a New York City murder that was watched by 38 witnesses, none of whom called the police because they did not want to become involved.[39]

The Messenger Effect   When the news media report stories that are important to a large number of people, researchers must look into the messenger
effect: whether, or to what extent, repercussions follow from the events or the
news stories about them. When the news media report an increase in inflation, the people who change their opinions about the president or alter their
economic behavior do so because of the event; the story is secondary.

Journalists play an active role in the messenger effects under two conditions. The first is when they are the messengers of news that would otherwise
not be known. In an era of many highly competitive news outlets, this happens rarely except when all journalists believe only a tiny and unrepresenta-
tive part of their total audience would be interested in the story.

Investigative reporters who obtain exposés report events that might otherwise go unnoticed, in which case they should be credited with messenger effects. In fact their colleagues make sure that they obtain credit because journalism's highest honors are very often awarded to investigative reporters.[40]

The second instance of active effects is when journalists depict an event so
as to maximize its attention-getting quality: story placement, length, or highlighting the story's most dramatic portions at the expense of possibly more
significant aspects.[41] Sometimes, the highlighting can have a considerable
messenger effect. Television reporting of the Selma and other civil rights
marches of the 1960s, which focused mainly on the southern sheriffs who attacked marchers with water hoses, cattle prods, and dogs, may have helped to
mobilize the popular support necessary for the subsequent passage of the era's
civil rights legislation.[42] At the very least it hastened the passage of the
legislation.

Such dramatic effects are rare, because usually the messengers are secondary to the events and statements they cover. Thus, Marshall McLuhan's
now-classic phrase, that the medium affects the message, is incomplete. The
messenger sometimes affects it as well, but much of the time the events themselves are the message.

Effects on Institutions and the Larger Society

The news media may actually affect institutions and organizations more frequently and strongly than they do news audiences. When institutions are in
the public eye and depend on voter, client, or customer goodwill, they seek
positive coverage and fear news that can endanger that goodwill. As a result,
they often react almost immediately to "bad" news and may alter their advertising and other public behavior in response to it.

Watchdog Effects   As I mentioned a number of times, journalists may have their greatest effect when they act as watchdogs, reporting illegal, dishonest, immoral, and other behavior violating mainstream norms. The watchdog story is basically a morality tale; not only of immorality discovered but of moral norms and standards preserved. Immense numbers of domestic news stories fall into this category because they report violations of laws or values, examples of unfairness, or of actions that may be legal but ought to be sanctioned, punished, or eliminated.

Whether the watchdog effect stems from investigative reporting or is a serendipitous result of legwork for a routine story, it is also the journalists' finest opportunity to show that they are working to advance democracy.[43] Whether or not they achieve their aim is another question, as most watchdog news has no visible effects, and sometimes, unintended effects turn out not to be democratic. The exposés of the "muckrakers" of the early twentieth century helped to bring about the Progressive movement but as Lincoln Steffens later discovered, its efficient, morally upstanding, and clean government not only achieved its intended aim of reducing the power of the urban political machine but also exacted heavy material and other costs on working-class and poor city dwellers.[44]

The watchdog effect works because large or widely respected institutions and organizations must protect their reputations. In public agencies, leaders and budgets may be endangered, especially if watchdog news has potentially negative consequences at the next election. Commercial firms can spend millions of dollars if and when enough news about an unsafe consumer product results in a sharp decline in business or leads to government investigations.[45] News about illegal or morally questionable decisions can, under some circumstances, hasten a firm's collapse, as the Enron and other scandals of 2002 illustrates.

Most watchdog stories are political because most news is political. Michael Schudson has rightly argued that the mere existence of the news media has an effect on politicians, who must always be aware of how journalists cover them just in case their constituents are paying attention.[46] The news media put politicians and political institutions on notice in several ways.

From day to day, the journalists' presence requires politicians and political organizations to be on their best public behavior, whether it pertains to manners or democratic norms. Politicians do not use profanity while journalists are taking notes, and the military does not commit atrocities in the vicinity of television cameras.[47] Exemplary behavior does not have the same effects, however. It is less often reported, but it may also be questioned by a cynical population that does not expect its public officials to be exemplary.

Best behavior also means avoidance of mistakes. President Gerald Ford's public failure to remember that Poland was behind the Iron Curtain hurt him considerably because it reinforced his opponents' claim that he lacked sufficient intelligence "to walk and chew gum at the same time." Subsequently, Dan Quayle's spelling deficiencies and the tangled syntax of the Presidents H.W. and G.W. Bush had the same result.[48]

Journalistic competition and other factors have fashioned news out of the deviant acts of politicians that were once suppressed by journalistic consensus. Extramarital affairs, alcoholism, and drug use sometimes have such an immediate effect that the offending public official resigns before the political damage is even known. Sometimes, however, the same activities are considered to have no visible effect, most likely because enough voters see enough redeeming features in the deviant actor to look the other way, as they did in Bill Clinton's case while he was president.[49]

Still, the most prevalent form of watchdog journalism remains journalists' never-ending search for villains. "60 Minutes" owes its success and longevity to the fact that it focuses on watchdog news.[50] Catching villains is not only more popular but has more immediate effects than identifying the institutional shortcomings that produce them.

Watchdog effects take place not only because exposés are conducted but because enough people in the news audience pay attention enough of the time, and thereby make elected officials take notice too. The journalists' effectiveness as messengers helps. Thus, a watchdog story in the New York Times almost always has more impact because it is in the Times rather than in a newspaper of lesser status, and because other newspapers may follow up the Times story. Meanwhile, government officials must investigate the story and try to put an end to the problems that result in negative publicity.[51]

Watchdog stories do not automatically result in watchdog effects, however. To start, the investigative reporting may be too brief to obtain enough attention-getting information, and the investigative reporters may not get enough help from other sources. Expecting one newspaper or magazine to develop an exposé of a giant organization single-handedly is unfair, and it rarely happens without cooperation from other agencies.

Further, the watchdog effect can be aborted because no influential audience is paying attention. If the citizenry is not sufficiently aroused by illegality and corruption, the journalists' message, even in the New York Times, falls on deaf ears. As the battles of the Progressive movement with big city machines demonstrated regularly, what the affluent classes condemn as corruption, the less than affluent treat as a source of jobs and of needed resources in lieu of jobs. Even now, exposés of excessive campaign contributions and outright political bribery, as well as legislative favors in return for them arouse little public anger.

Moreover, the effectiveness of watchdog stories in stimulating change is limited by the journalists' and the audience's greater interest in finding and punishing villains than in identifying systemic, and thus impersonal short-comings. If villains are powerful enough they may escape punishment, and even if they are punished, they may be replaced by new villains. Changing arrangements and institutions so that incentives and rewards for villainous behavior are terminated is both more difficult and less glamorous.

When public officials are forced to make regulatory decisions that have costly consequences, incentives to bribe the regulators are inevitable. If build-ing inspections are delayed, builders for whom time is always money find it cheaper to pay inspectors to move them up in the waiting line than to wait their turn for inspections. The payoffs may be cheaper for the city too, because hiring more building inspectors to speed up inspections is expensive.

The costs of political change, particularly for powerful "vested interests" and the amount of money at stake for those exposed by the watchdogs are es-pecially relevant. Even the most dramatic investigative reporting is unlikely to have results if large quantities of public or private monies are at stake, or if major expenditures of political capital are needed, or a shift in political power arrangements is threatened. In that case, the villains fingered in the watch-dog stories are apt to wait and see if the anticipated public disapproval actu-ally takes place, and even to wait until critics and reformers tire and the status quo ante can be reestablished.

Despite noble efforts by a few reporters and newspapers to report exten-sively on job downsizing when it first became newsworthy in the early 1990s, neither the government nor private industry altered its jobs policies signifi-cantly before they were both rescued by the economic boom of the late 1990s.[52] The many investigations of Florida voting and vote counting after the 2000 elections did not reverse the election results, and even the push toward elec-tion reforms lasted only a few months. The voting machinery was identified as the villain, but nothing was done to guarantee citizens that polling places would be open and their votes declared valid. People are often angered by a good exposé but not always in large enough numbers or long enough to bring about change.

Institutions can protect themselves from watchdog effects in other ways, for example by moving offending behavior "backstage," where journalists can-not see it. During the Gulf War, the Pentagon imposed rigid control of the news media, thus preventing journalists from discovering, among other things, that the Pentagon's "smart" weapons were not so smart.[53] Although correspondents were often limited to reporting the Pentagon's version of the war, they also made it very clear to their audiences that the Pentagon was restricting them.[54]

Watchdogs probably have the most dramatic effects in totalitarian nations, where the secret police can terrorize, imprison, or murder journalists seeking to expose the regime. The underground press that frequently springs up in these countries can sometimes undertake investigative journalism with more potent results, for example, in obtaining a large and loyal audience, than in democratic societies. True, there is far more to investigate, and the citizenry is almost totally dependent on the underground press for honest reporting. Totalitarian regimes can close down the offending newspaper or television station and arrest the journalists, but when a large proportion of the citizenry wants to hear the watchdogs' message, totalitarian regimes become fearful of losing the complete control they believe they need to stay in power.

General Political Effects   The news media also have regular and routine political effects.[55] Such effects are difficult to identify, however, because journalists play, and have long played, major roles in communicating governmental and political events and statements, and are thus in some respects a part of government and politics rather than outside it. For example, journalists ensure that the political process is always visible, keeping it on the public agenda and urging often uninterested people to continue to pay attention to it.

In addition, journalists help inform the citizen lobbies, research organizations, and other monitors of what transpires above and below the radar. Concurrently, these groups supply journalists with the information and leads they collect during their monitoring and other activities.[56]

Public officials do not necessarily agree that journalists are an intrinsic part of government and politics. They often consider newspeople to be outsiders, and hostile ones at that. Nonetheless, public officials also need journalists and therefore try to shape the events they control and the statements they make to fit the needs of both the journalists and the audience. Public officials and the news media use each other in a sufficient number of ways that a cause-effects model cannot easily be applied to the symbiotic relationship that is at times also a set of feedback loops.

One example of the symbiosis is the leak. Officials leak ostensibly secret information, for example about future legislation, to journalists as trial balloons, enabling the officials to test reactions to it. Conversely, officials hostile to the legislation may also leak information in hopes of generating enough political opposition so that the legislation will never see the light of day. Officials also use the news media to send messages to higher-level offices of the government, because once the messages are public, their recipients can ignore them less easily than a memo sent through official channels. Leaks are particularly attractive to reporters especially if they can persuade the leakers to give them exclusives that can be used to scoop their competitors.[57]

The news media as a whole may have their greatest impact as contributors to a mysterious and sometimes ephemeral causal force called the political climate or the political mood that is perceived by elected officials and then affects their decisions and other actions. The climate is in effect an indicator of policy changes or other political actions the "public," itself a mysterious aggregation, thinks ought to be undertaken or halted. Political observers thought to have their fingers on the public pulse infer the climate from materials supplied largely by the news media: stories, editorials, columns, letters, and polls that elected officials and their staffs interpret to construct the climate.[58] Climate shifts are inferred from new subjects showing up in a news stories, changing answers to standard polling questions or noticeable increases in letters to the editors on particular topics. In the absence of political obligations or requests from campaign funders, party leaders, and other important supporters, elected officials may be guided by what they see as and in the political climate. If they deem the climate to be sufficiently turbulent, pacifying it may take precedence over all other priorities.

The climate is also ephemeral, however, because often no one can quite "see" it. Sometimes, powerful public officials can decide that a climate exists, that enables them to demand or carry out policies they support. Whether they have evidence of such a climate or just manufacture it is another question, but if the officials involved are powerful enough, they can get away with what they have done.

Related political effects takes place because the news media help to assemble the audiences whose opinions play various roles in the political process and are incorporated in the political climate. To be sure, the news media cannot control their audience and may not even be able to attract their attention to political news, but public officials must nevertheless act as if an audience is paying attention.

Officials even treat the news media's attention to them as an indication that the audience is ready to pay attention, believing that journalists would not include stories about the officials' activities if people were not interested.

Indeed, public officials often ascribe magical effects to the news media, particularly the television cameras, and try their best to appear in front of them. Being written about on page one of a major newspaper does not hurt either. Actually, the White House makes sure, to the extent it can, that it appears on network television and in the national newspapers every day, preferably with the "message" it has prepared for that day.

For the less powerful, an appearance on the network evening news, or a front-page story in the *New York Times* or *Washington Post* offers a rare opportunity for national visibility, but even more so, to demonstrate the potential power inherent in that appearance. If journalists, who are not political players, recognize a public official as important, that official must have some power or influence, and the political players act accordingly.

In theory, the news media could choose their news stories in order to deliberately bestow such power, but they do not. As professionals working in a competitive commercial milieu, they must choose their stories using journalistic criteria. However, the choices they make on professional and commercial grounds are given political meaning by others and can at times initiate power shifts that influence political decisions. Eventually, however, media exposure has its limits. If media-hungry politicians do not ultimately deliver, they are eventually dismissed as camera hogs even by the audience.[59]

What happens in the centers of power is far from the districts where citizens actually live. As a result, citizens are background figures and walk-ons in photo ops, to be noticed otherwise mainly when they protest, and when citizen groups achieve political victories. Perhaps the low level of journalistic attention paid to citizens has depressed their level of political activity. But it is hard to imagine that many citizens would be politically active just to get their names in the papers.

Because the news media are so visible, especially to media researchers, it is easy to exaggerate their political effects. It is also easy to forget that politics and government are not about communication but about money and power. The news media do not often mention it, but governments are embedded in a national power structure in which political, economic, and other organizations and forces struggle for scarce material and nonmaterial resources. In this structure, the news media are an always visible but a rarely influential player.[60]

Electoral Effects   The news media see elections as central to American democracy and themselves as the prime facilitators of electoral communication, but their effects on election outcomes are less significant than commonly thought.[61] For one thing, except at the presidential level, many incumbents are reelected without doing much communicating of any kind. Moreover, in many elections, a large number of voters make up their minds about their presidential choices before the serious campaigning begins. In addition, hand-shaking continues to be a significant campaign activity, and local political organizations and unions still work hard to get voters to the polls.[62] Only in close elections are journalists major players.

The news media coverage virtually ignores these political facts of life, however, and journalists treat election campaigns as lengthy contests between candidates to get their messages and personas across to the entire electorate. The role of the news media in elections even appears to be declining. They once had a near monopoly in reporting them, but today's campaigns concentrate increasingly on political advertising and "debates" between the major candidates, neither of which are controlled by the news media.

True, the news media still supply the traditional daily reports from the campaign trail and regular roundups of the horse races, but their major contribution, particularly on the part of television, may be to provide prospective voters with the opportunity to see the candidates in order to evaluate their "character."[63] The daily stories become almost ritualistic, however, and candidates try to find ways of upstaging their opponents to create memorable moments hoping to leave an impression on voters. Presidential campaigns use investigative committees to look for scandals or mistakes that might illustrate their opponents' inability to be presidential. The news media function mainly as messengers in this competition, often depending on information supplied by the opposing campaigns. Journalists are often moderators of the increasingly important debates, but the candidates negotiate the formats of the debates, and often the moderators cannot even ask their own questions.[64] Besides, the debaters generally answer most questions with excerpts from their stump speeches.

The news media do not play a role in the creation of campaign advertising, except insofar as ads are sometimes modeled on or inspired by news stories. However, when ads become controversial, journalists turn them into news stories, which at times can considerably increase the number of people who see the ads. By now, wily campaign consultants have learned to create controversial ads to be shown only in television news stories, turning the networks and cable channels into involuntary participants in the campaigns.

The greater role of campaign advertising in elections has itself had an important effect, but one that is also beyond the journalists' control. Media advertising is expensive, television ads cost more than other kinds, and the prices television stations charge to run them are on the whole higher than the prices they charge for other ads. Someone has to pay the bills, and those who do so are empowered to have an effect on government and politics.[65]

Visibility Effects   One of the news media's general effects is to provide frequent visibility to elected officials and their other regular sources. Although everyone is allegedly entitled to 15 minutes of such visibility, those already in the public eye tend to get more attention than others. So, of course, do people who are elected to or otherwise chosen for high-profile roles.

That fame is measured in minutes rather than inches indicates indirectly that television does more for visibility than the print media. Although being on page one of the national newspapers or on the cover of the major news magazines still provides prestigious visibility, the proliferation of television news programs, and their practice of repeating news stories and rerunning tapes, keeps a handful of national leaders in front of the public almost 24 hours a day.[66]

The news media also make the country as a whole visible to its audience, providing it with a different picture than they get from their own family histories, vacation trips, and the like. Although the national news media try hard to cover as many parts of and places in the country as possible, most domestic news is about Washington, D.C., and a handful of other big cities and states. More important perhaps, the American news audience learns something about other countries, and because American newspapers, magazines, and television news programs are often sent overseas, other countries learn about the United States. Sometimes, these exchanges can produce political effects.[67]

A good example of such an effect is the ability of round-the-clock television programs and internet websites to supply news from all over the world, and sometimes more quickly than the federal government's intelligence-gathering agencies. As a result, the government may have to react before it has had time to consult with relevant government advisers and to consider alternative policies.[68]

Scapegoating Effects   While shedding light on American politics, the news media also shed more light on themselves. Journalists have sometimes been treated as biased messengers for reporting news people did not want to hear, notably at the beginning of the Watergate scandal. But in the process they have also become scapegoats, blamed for the emergence of social changes and new values of which significant or vocal numbers in the news audience disapproved. Whether they are accused of covering evolution at the expense of creationism or supporting the greater tolerance its opponents call "moral relativism," the fault is often assigned to "the media."

The scapegoating extends both to entertainment and news media. The entertainment media are probably held most responsible for alleged effects associated with sex and violence, permissiveness, and other deviations from perceived traditional norms, especially adults' norms for children. The news media are more often blamed for political and economic transformations: both for encouraging globalization and supplying publicity for protesters against globalization who would otherwise remain dormant.

The Right blames liberals and the Left for having bewitched the news media to help it take over the country from what the Right sees as the conservative majority; the Left sees journalists as caving in to the flood of proposals and publicity put forth by right-wing foundations on behalf of the corporate world or the religious and other social conservatives.[69] Liberals rightly point out that the conservatives can afford to create information and hire spokespeople for which liberals lack funds.

Politicians scapegoat the news media for somewhat the same limitation: their inability to persuade the country of their proposals and positions. A significant number of elected officials believe that if their positions or ideas were less simplified and more fully reported, the country's affairs would be run more liberally, or conservatively, or just more effectively. In effect, politicians blame the news media for not generating the political support they themselves cannot obtain.

Judging by the polls, many people are unaware of the exact boundaries between the news and the entertainment media and can therefore combine them into the general media scapegoat.[70] Because the media remains undefined, it is impossible to determine which specific media, if any, are being scapegoated. The mass media may not even be the scapegoat, but a powerful symbol for all the actual and imagined outsiders that threaten the people who consider themselves the insiders, and the rightful controllers of the country's culture and institutions.[71] The media could even be a secular devil for our times.

When the media of people's imaginations as well as the actual news media, are used as scapegoats, they create further political and cultural effects. By absorbing accusations, the scapegoated media may help take the blame off the institutions and individuals that would otherwise have been accused. Politicians, bureaucrats, racial and sexual minorities, the poor, and others might be scapegoated even more widely and intensely were the media not available.

Whatever effects the media are accused of, they are no doubt blamed in part because they are a particularly safe target. Neither the entertainment nor news media often complain publicly, rarely sue, and refrain from using their influence in Washington to obtain protection from their accusers. As commercial firms, they use that influence primarily to expand their markets and increase their profits.

The Possibility of Long-Range Effects

On the whole, the news media's effects are limited, but there may yet be long-range, even permanent effects of the news media that are not apparent or directly traceable to them. Although many observers and critics of the news media believe that such effects must exist because the media are always around us, the currently available research methodology cannot detect them, if they actually do exist.

Perhaps future research methods will pick up current but now invisible long-range effects, and perhaps some will emerge when television news and the internet have been here longer.[72] For example, new reactions, such as increased tolerance for harmless others can perhaps be traced at least partly to the news media. Also, television, including television news has frequently been accused of shortening American attention spans.[73]

Still, if America's news media had significant long-range effects, one would think that some would by now have been identified. The mass-circulation press has been around for more than 150 years, and even the half-hour network television news programs have been broadcast every weekday evening for 40 years. Admittedly, a number of scholars and other observers, beginning with Marshall McLuhan, have identified long-range effects of television, but they have not supplied enough persuasive evidence of the existence of these effects.[74]

The reverse hypothesis, that the news media are themselves effects of larger changes in American society must also be considered. These media came into being with other "modern" institutions and would not exist apart from them; in addition, changes in the media might be driven by other forms of societal change.[75] In that case, the effects on the news media must somehow be separated from the effects of these media.

What Journalists Can and Cannot Do for Democracy

The news is essential to democracy and as my thought experiment earlier in the chapter suggests, under some conditions, the absence of journalists could lead to autocracy or chaos. Watchdog journalism can contribute information to help keep public officials honest and, at times, even encourage them to be more responsive to their constituents. The journalists' theory of democracy has it right, however; their main power is to inform the citizenry. Others will have to persuade the citizenry to be better informed.

At times, journalists can tell people what to think about, and perhaps even make them think, although thinking per se does not lead to action. If enough people are thinking along the same line and are actively making their thoughts known, they can affect the political climate that influences the actions of political leaders.

Even so, journalists by themselves cannot make people act, nor can they make people's actions have political consequences. Instead, journalists' principal effects are as messengers. Sometimes, the right message, carried by the right messenger at the right time can instigate action. Journalist Dwight Mac-Donald's *New Yorker* article about Michael Harrington's book, *The Other America* helped move President Kennedy to start the War on Poverty.[76] But neither journalists nor anyone else can predict what messages will have such an effect.

Now mainly messengers for high government officials, journalists could also be messengers for citizens seeking to strengthen democracy. The news media supply visibility and could in theory spread such visibility to other than the major political leaders. Making public figures visible does not require others to see them, however, and besides, visibility is not power.

Journalists can turn the activities of powerful business people and firms into news and even into exposés, but neither news nor exposés alone can reduce their economic or political power. The same goes for the power of other organizations. News supplies information but citizens and politicians have to bring about greater democracy. Journalists should not kid themselves into thinking they can turn news into power.[77] These observations inspire the suggestions for change that take up the remaining two chapters of the book.

CHAPTER 5

The News: What Might Be Done

We have seen that the news has a number of significant effects, beginning with the creation of social continuity, as well as messenger, watchdog, and a number of political effects on and for American democracy. To be sure, the effects of the news are limited; consequently, the extent to which journalists can help strengthen the democratic roles and powers of the citizenry is also limited. If nothing else, journalists may be able to help citizens increase their understanding of the democracy within which they now live, in the world of the twenty-first century. In any case, it is worth asking what journalists could do differently or better; how they might change the news on behalf of the citizenry.

The very notion of changing the news may seem like a pipe dream in an era in which the news audience has been shrinking, journalists have often been downsized, and many news firms have cut other costs in order to increase their rates of profit. But challenging times can sometimes spur thinking about change.

The suggestions that follow are illustrative not comprehensive. Indeed, I have focused mainly on suggestions that might enable journalists to be politically and otherwise more useful to their audience, with the ultimate aim of enhancing the citizens' role in the country's politics.[1] Several of the suggestions have been made before and some are already in use here and there.

These suggestions are meant to complement today's news, and they range from the practical to the ideal. Although some are relevant for all news media, others are most suitable for the national print media that are large and well staffed, enabling them to experiment and see what works.

User-Friendly News

In order to consider how journalists might strengthen the citizenry, they need to figure out how to bring more readers back to the news, including those who now get their news mainly from 60-second or 250-word news bulletins. Even in a period of declining audiences, news buffs by definition remain loyal. The journalistic challenge is to involve more of the audience in political and economic news, to woo back as much of the departed news audience as possible, and to attract at least some of the young adults who never even joined the audience. In short, the news media have to be friendly to the users in order to persuade the users to be friendly toward the news.

One way of achieving both goals is to make a serious attempt to discover what audiences think they need to know, to add what journalists think they need to know, and to structure the reporting and presentation of news accordingly. To put it in terms of a basic professional dichotomy, user friendliness requires journalists to make what they consider important news sufficiently interesting to the audience, and to make room also for news that audiences consider important or interesting. In addition, journalists ought to recognize people's need to be known, as it were, especially to government. As I suggested earlier, journalists should make news out of what people deem to be major issues, especially unattended ones.

Although the news media collect endless data about audience size and characteristics, data needed to develop user friendliness is scarce. If journalists wish to understand audience needs, they must know more about topics such as how and why people now "use" the news, what various kinds of news mean in their lives, what the audience is doing when it is "keeping up" with the news, and when it is most engaged with a story.

In short, audience research should be focused on how to make the news more user-friendly. By this criterion, the current audience studies that ask people overly simple and very general questions about their opinions are nearly completely useless. Standard polls should be replaced with intensive interviews, or better still, with informal observation and discussion with people about the role that news plays or could play in their lives.

Although some of this research can be left to researchers, journalists should, whenever and wherever possible, gather their own answers as well. They need the opportunity to spend time and speak informally with all parts of their news audience.

These opportunities are virtually absent from the journalistic experience. Unlike many other professionals, journalists spend most of their time with their suppliers, that is their sources, and even then, they are now mostly on the telephone. As a result, they are largely deprived of the informal, wide-ranging audience contact that academic researchers enjoy with their students, or doctors with their patients. Journalists appear to talk informally mostly with each other.[2]

In recent years a number of newspapers have appointed staff members to listen to and speak with readers, including dissatisfied ones who canceled their subscriptions. They then pass on the results of their audience contact to colleagues in the newsroom.[3] In an ideal world the contact should begin much earlier. Journalism schools should offer courses in which students spend time talking with people in the news audience, and then write reports on how and what types of news they would deliver to the audience members they have met.[4] News organizations could provide a similar opportunity for new hires as well as long-term employees, including executives.

"Living with the audience" experiences can help journalists keep an audience in mind once they go to work in professional news organizations. They might also become more sensitive to audience perceptions of the news, their criteria of newsworthiness, and how the audience frames the events that journalists turn into news.

Visiting journalists should be encouraged to learn something about what I earlier called "folk journalism;" what lay people do when they act as journalists, telling familial and other everyday news to each other, and the methods they use to encourage their audiences to become informed. Professional journalists might be able to take some lessons back to their newsrooms.

There are many other requirements for making news more user-friendly, such as correcting the shortcomings of the news cited in studies of the audience. For example, journalists need to become more familiar with what news audiences view as inaccuracies in the news, what they misunderstand or fail to understand, and what they do not want to understand. Above all, however, journalists must learn the various ways in which people inform themselves and become informed: how they access the news they want or think they need to know.[5]

The remainder of this chapter is devoted to specific suggestions about news that might encourage citizens to inform themselves more adequately than they do now, particularly about topics that would enable them to seek a greater role in American democracy. The suggestions are not presented in order of importance.

Localizing National and International News

Almost every audience study indicates that people are more interested in local than national and international news, except when world-shaking events take place. By localizing the news I mean turning international and national news into local stories by reporting the effects, implications, and impacts of what happens in the larger world for the local community. Localizing might make national and overseas news more relevant to, and thus more user-friendly for, the news audience.

Localized news reporting would trace the known and likely consequences of a national event or statement to the locality, and to as many of the local institutions and residents touched by it as possible. Localized news already exists, for example when a national manufacturing company announces factory closings. Then, the local news media usually spell out the implications of the closing for the locality, from major victims to plans for replacing the departed employer.[6]

International events should also be localized, for many have local connections, even if they are not immediately apparent. Today, most international news is domestic news about Americans making news overseas, whether as soldiers, victims of terrorism, or lawbreakers. Truly foreign news is scarce, probably because much of it has no immediate impact on most Americans. But if journalists learned more about the indirect consequences, international events could be made more meaningful.

For example, the genocides across the former Yugoslavia and the Afghanistan wars could have been reported in much greater detail if they had been localized, and connected to the refugees who ended up as American immigrants and moved into American cities.

Actually, most national news is an abstraction; journalists create one national story about events and statements that may have different consequences for various sectors of the country. The president of the United States may act as the president of all the people, but his actions will have different meanings and implications across the country. Many White House stories affect Californians one way and New Yorkers another way. Ups and downs in the rates of unemployment and inflation are national stories because the government reports them that way, but what people experience are the local rates of each. Localized news thus concretizes the abstraction.

In a globalized world where the economic life of an American community will be increasingly altered by decisions of the European Union or a Korean cartel, many more localized news stories will have to be reported, and with greater depth than today. Localizing the news is not easy, however. Tracing indirect effects requires a combination of local, national, and international expertise not often found among journalists, and the analysis of long-range effects requires some speculation. Localizing is also expensive, especially if and when it calls for local journalists to do legwork away from their home base. Alternatively, local, national, and overseas journalists may have to work together, requiring bureaucratic and other innovations. An easier solution might be to establish specialist news organizations that can work with affected localities to localize stories. Syndicated coverage is particularly relevant when national or international events affect a number of localities similarly at the same time.

Localizing need not only be spatial, however, as audiences might become more interested in the news if journalists reduced the gap between national or local news and the personal needs and interest of the audience. Journalists sometimes already do so half-heartedly, but the main focus of national news is usually on the national story; local and personal implications are reported as afterthought. Ideally, the emphasis should be reversed, because the big story is actually in the personal impact of the national story on the major sectors of the local news audience. The national legislation should be the afterthought. If journalists could upend the conventional emphasis, the news audience might become aware earlier when their elected representatives cut taxes that benefit mostly the very wealthy, or when Medicare reform does more for hospitals and drug manufacturers than for patients.

Participatory News

Believing that citizen participation is essential to democracy, journalists supply news they think will help citizens participate in politics. However, much of the news being from and about public officials, it has little to say about where, if anywhere citizens fit in. Journalists are not even likely to report if and when public officials try to limit citizen attendance or discourage active participation at public meetings—especially if these are standard public meeting procedures as they too often are.

The conventional top-down news coverage I discussed in Chapter 3 should be balanced by participatory news, news designed to provide direct or indirect aid to citizens who wish to participate or know how others are participating. Participatory news is not advocacy and does not require journalists to take sides or to violate the rules of journalistic objectivity.[7]

As I have noted previously, citizens usually become newsworthy when they come in unusual numbers or behave in unusual ways. Even then, the story is not why they are actively participating and what policies they are advocating, but the possibility that they are making "trouble" for public officials. Sometimes, journalists even seem disappointed when there is no trouble—and thus no story.[8] In any case, then journalists treat participators as deviants rather than as citizens, and whether they intend to or not, the news media discourage participation more than they encourage it.

Participatory news requires a reversal of these practices and should rest on the assumption that citizens are as relevant and important as public officials. Because citizens rarely attend public meetings, journalists must emphasize other, less public forms of citizen participation, such as stories about the topics of people's letters, e-mails, and calls to public officials.[9] What citizens say to the White House, the leaders of the Senate and House, and to their own elected officials deserves regular reporting.[10] The citizenry should also know who is conducting organized letter-writing campaigns, e-mailing, and phone calling, on what subjects and with what kind of turnout.

The informal political life of citizens is another source of participatory news. People engage in political discussions with family, friends, and neighbors, and in internet chat rooms, all of which provide raw material for news stories about citizen participation. Actually, journalists already do so when they hang out in New Hampshire coffee shops in the early weeks of the presidential primary season, but why stop then. Even the most commonly repeated political jokes are newsworthy, in part because they are more participatory than the monologues and cartoons of the professionals that appear in the news media.

These kinds of stories tell citizens in the news audience that other people are thinking and talking about politics, as well as what they are thinking and talking about. Such stories, properly written, inform citizens about each other more effectively than poll results.

Participatory journalism should also include news that is directly helpful in mobilizing citizens.[11] Local news media should take the opportunity to report on proposed or ongoing participatory activities, and where such activities are taking place. If demonstrations are planned, logistical information about where people are meeting, as well as phone numbers and websites that supply information can be reported without taking sides. If the strategies available to professional politicians are newsworthy, so are the strategies open to citizens.

Participatory news reporting should also help citizens find out what situations require their participation, and enable them to decide what if anything they want to do. Journalists cannot tell people to participate, even if they now do so indirectly by calling attention to injustice and corruption, or to attacks on citizen interests. However, they can report what citizens can do and what citizens have done in other places. Citizen successes are already reported from time to time, but failures, and the reasons for them also belong in participatory journalism. News stories about defective public services, public malfeasance, and the like are already standard, but they can be reframed to tell citizens what rights and powers they have to act, and experts could be interviewed to suggest strategies.

The defects and malfeasances of private enterprise and of nonprofit agencies could be reported in the same way. *Consumer Reports* and similar publications already do some of the investigative research, albeit for a small audience, but larger news audiences should be informed about what citizens have done, or could do, to complain, or what they need to know in order to act. The news media now supply news stories about these topics when new legislation is debated or when private firms come into conflict with the federal government, but in the everyday world, people experience problems with public agencies and private firms all the time, and reporting them would be newsworthy. Inside the beltway problems may make more exciting reading, but most people have to deal with routine problems most of the time.

A rather different approach to participatory news is a national adaptation of the old "action-line" columns that carried—and still do in many places— letters of complaint from citizens who were ill served by public agencies and commercial firms.[12] Sometimes, publication of the letters, and their potential to affect the reputations of the named firms and agencies, was enough to obtain redress, but if not the newspaper was ready to step in to make sure that justice prevailed. In a sense, action lines are watchdog journalism for citizens. The lines not only represent the people who are not very good at participating, but they enable the news media to undertake a nearly cost-free and populist form of investigative journalism. Even though they produce direct results only for aggrieved individuals, they mobilize others to get in touch. Indeed, action lines often develop a following that becomes a constituency to which wise public officials pay attention.

While action lines are traditionally associated with small-town and downscale local media, particularly newspapers, they can easily be adapted to national news media as well, including electronic and digital. In a society of federal agencies and national chain stores, action lines that appear in national media are a visible way of bringing in the citizenry.

Well-known network news correspondents who interview people with popular complaints against federal agencies could be very effective and might attract a large audience, especially if the cameras are present when complainants obtain justice.[13] If public officials are asked to be there as well, few will turn down an invitation that enables them to demonstrate to a national audience their ability to obtain satisfaction for complaining citizens.

Participatory news should include the downsides of citizen activity, however: for example, the difficulties of effective participation by amateurs. To the extent that journalists share responsibility for the myth that the essence of democracy is participation, they must also report the obstacles to implementing the myth and the illusions behind it.

The most serious downside of participatory news may be the additional help it would give citizens who need the least help—the more educated, politically active, and best-represented citizens. Journalists should not worsen the political inequality of those who are so inarticulate or invisible, or so preoccupied with daily survival crises that they are now left out of participatory activities altogether. But what if some journalists started writing stories in which they seek out and give voice to the least represented and most invisible?

Participatory News and "Public Journalism"

"Public journalism" is an ongoing reform movement within journalism in which journalists carry out special, and sometimes innovative, newsgathering and related information supplying projects to shed new light on community issues and to help the community identify and solve community problems.[14] For example, local newspapers might assemble special series on racial discrimination, juvenile delinquency, or school violence. News organizations that embrace public journalists also supply extra information to prospective voters in local elections, try to improve communication between citizens, as well as between citizens and elected officials, and between citizens and journalists. The notion of public journalism is broad enough to encourage many other projects, almost all informational projects oriented toward civic goals.[15]

Public journalists go public particularly at election time, but also when significant issues arise in the community.[16] Public journalists try to avoid controversy and partisan politics, and in one famous case, a local election-time survey of community issues was so careful to be nonpartisan that it inadvertently overlooked major issues being raised by the candidates.[17]

In fact, public journalism privileges mainstream issues, prefers mild controversies, and is unlikely to go beyond the ideological margins of conventional journalism. In contrast, I see participatory journalism as more citizen oriented, taking a political, and when necessary, adversarial, view of the citizen-official relationship.

Explanatory Journalism

Journalism is in many respects a moral enterprise, dedicated to reporting injustice and ethical wrongdoing. But until morality becomes a major engine of social change, journalists must also undertake explanatory journalism, providing hard-headed and tough-minded explanations of why political, economic, and other institutions and their leaders act as they do.

As my label suggests, explanatory journalism seeks first and foremost to answer "why" questions: to report why the events and statements described by conventional journalism took place. Less broad in scope than what journalists call analytic or interpretive journalism, explanatory journalism has two prime purposes.[18] One is to help people understand what is happening to them and the country, and to identify the reasons for and the causes of what is happening. A second purpose is to provide explanatory information about conditions that citizens want to eliminate, helping them understand what reforms and structural changes must be undertaken. Knowing why things are as they are and what shores up the status quo will help people figure out what political and other strategies might lead to the reforms they seek.[19]

"Why stories" are vital and when visible, unusual changes take place in public life as well as private institutions, and people want to understand the effects of these changes on them. If explanations are not forthcoming and enough people become anxious, rumors and paranoid theories may spring up to answer the why questions instead.[20]

The demand for explanation is also likely to increase as the world becomes more interdependent. For example, unless and until enough Americans understand why our foreign policies generate the hatred they do in some parts of the world, terrorism cannot end. Connecting this hatred to American policies will generate patriotic anger, which can only be defused, if at all, by equally patriotic but sensitive journalism.[21]

In addition, explanatory journalism can strengthen watchdog journalism. I suggested in Chapter 4 that investigative reporting that exposes villains should explain the conditions that make villainous behavior possible, and thereby help prevent the opportunity for new villains to appear after the exposés have been forgotten.

A number of journalists question the desirability or the possibility of explanatory journalism, suggesting that their job, already difficult enough, is to report the "facts" and to do so accurately and truthfully.[22] Some journalists see themselves as supplying "context," the groups and activities within which events take place and statements are made. Others stick with the time-honored practice of speculating, particularly about the self-seeking motives of politicians.[23]

The resort to speculation is understandable, for explanatory journalism is difficult to do. Explaining that an elected official's actions in office are motivated by his or her next reelection campaign is easy, and therefore becomes virtually a standard guess. Discovering why things happen as they do cannot usually be done by contacting the standard sources. Experienced beat reporters may be able to supply explanations, for they know how the agencies and people they report function, have ideas about why, and may be in touch with the experts and researchers who have done more systematic explanatory work.

Explanatory journalists face another task: to translate their legwork and other research into language lay people can understand, and into stories that will interest them. Putting explanatory journalism on television is harder yet. Even in the past, when news budgets were larger, few television beat reporters and, for that matter, documentarians, had enough time to do serious explanatory journalism. Causes cannot always be transformed into visuals for television, which helps to keep why stories off the small screen in the first place.[24]

Because of the obstacles that face both print and electronic news media, most explanatory journalism has been carried out by book-writing journalists who have time to explore and research all the possible leads. They also have the time to find the experts who are trained to dig for causes and are willing and able to work with journalists.[25] Book-length projects usually take so much time that freelance authors have to limit themselves to past events that still evoke reader interest and sell books years later.[26] Even then, authors can reach only a small part of the news audience.

The most logical way to funnel explanatory journalism to the regular news audience is to train beat writers in explanatory journalism for the major beats. Generalists who can do legwork among the most expert explainers would cover topics that fall outside the beats.

Opinions and "News Opinions"

Although most news audience studies suggest that people want journalists to stick to the facts, a case can be made for the opposite position: that the news media include more opinions. I offer at least two reasons. First, opinions are desirable when journalists who have done a lot of legwork develop informed opinions, and these ought to be shared with the news audience.[27]

The dictates of objectivity have required journalists to eschew explicit opinions, which are then left to colleagues on the editorial page and to columnists, op-ed contributors, and letter writers. Most of these opinion makers, notably columnists, are generalists, however, and their level of expertise on specific topics may not differ much from either general reporters or the lay audience. Nonetheless, they must constantly comment on an ongoing variety of subjects. Some opinion makers do legwork on the subjects about which they opine, but others pass on what they already know, which can at times include the myths and stereotypes of the moment.[28]

Consequently, "generalist" opinion needs to be complemented by what I think of as "news opinion." I resort to this word purposely because the opinions have to come from, and be limited to, beat and other reporters who have already done the necessary legwork for their news stories and are informed about their subjects. Now, these journalists may sometimes be asked to add news analyses or interpretive news stories, but they are usually still required to exclude their opinions. Were they able to inject their opinions, they could apply their personal judgment to their reportage and analyses, enabling them to evaluate what they have reported. The result would be informed opinion, and if reporters with different perspectives and values were asked to supply it, and their differences were explained, the news audience would benefit from the resulting diversity.

The second reason for the inclusion of opinions is that journalists often insert opinions into their stories already, even if they usually do so unintentionally. Conversely, sometimes opinions appear because journalists hold them so firmly that they confuse them with facts. Indeed, permitting explicit opinions may help journalists see how often they now add implicit ones. When journalists see racial minorities playing a "race card," but do not mention that whites opposing affirmative action may be doing the same, when business writers who report the decisions of executives and then write about workers as labor, and when political reporters identify protesters as "radical elements," they are expressing opinions. When journalists write about what the "American people" want or what the "public" thinks, and say so without any empirical evidence, they are only offering their own opinion—and turning it into an imagined national consensus at the same time.

Journalists trained to concentrate on the facts may need some help in learning how to add opinions based on their legwork.[29] Complementing straight stories with opinion should, in the print media, result in additional letters from readers, as well as criticism from advertisers and others from time to time. This is another reason to supply a diversity of opinions whenever possible.[30] The diversity requirement would also put further pressure on news organizations to correct present imbalances of race, class, and other characteristics in the roster of journalists.

In addition to news-opinions, the news media could use more opinion in general, from the news audience, professional journalists, and others. More opinion can be created by a larger number of op-ed pages and letter columns.[31] Both might be supplemented by modern versions of "people on the street" columns and television programs. Admittedly, internet chat rooms and websites already give voice to large numbers of individuals who offer even larger numbers of opinions, but the news media would concentrate on opinions about currently newsworthy subjects. These opinion formats could also be used to give a voice to the unheard-from populations whose views are not likely to be represented by editorial, op-ed, and letter writers.

In addition, the inclusion of more opinions across the ideological and other spectra would supply audiences with ideas they might not otherwise encounter. Equally important, enlarging the range and number of opinions is ultimately the only way the news media can achieve the balance they need to be perceived as free from bias. The practice of assuming that there are only two sides, or opinions, on major issues and that a balance is achieved by mentioning both, may save space or airtime but it cannot do justice to the diversity of opinion among the citizenry.

A democratic polity needs the largest variety of opinions—and of proposed solutions—to significant issues. That some opinions may be represented by very small constituencies is far less relevant in the media than in politics. Good ideas often come from the margins.

Admittedly, adding more opinions has downsides as well: too many opinions can devalue individual ones, or load up the political discourse with more diversity than it can handle. A larger number of opinions will surely encourage some holders of opinion to shout theirs even more loudly than is the case today. But the downsides do not diminish the virtues of adding opinions.

The addition of news opinion and the increase in opinion per se might, when combined with the opinions collected by pollsters, even provide the "public sphere" that some theorists of democracy advocate as a vessel of public debate. Whether a public sphere exists actually or even symbolically is unclear.[32] Whether it should exist needs discussion, for without a constitutional provision for such a sphere, the voices of the citizenry could be replaced.

Multiperspectival News and News Media

Differences in opinion are often the result of seeing the same phenomenon from several perspectives. The same observation applies to news, requiring what I have previously called "multiperspectival" news and news media.[33] Ideally, multiperspectival news encompasses fact and opinion reflecting all possible perspectives. In practice, it means making a place in the news for presently unrepresented viewpoints, unreported facts, and unrepresented, or rarely reported, parts of the population.[34]

To put it another way, multiperspectival news is the bottoms-up corrective for the mostly top-down perspectives of the news media that I described in Chapter 3. However, while the top may be small, no single bottoms-up perspective exists. The country is comprised of many bottoms, or publics, each with its own conception of the proper ways of looking at the world, about what the facts are, and which facts are relevant to a story or issue.[35] The first priority, and by now an old one, is to eliminate the continuing racial and class biases in the news, so that ethnic and racial minorities, as well as moderate- and low-income people are no longer viewed through the lenses of white and elite stereotypes or reported on only when they turn their back on mainstream ways or commit crimes.[36] Exemplary though it was, the 2000 *New York Times* series, "How Race is Lived in America," which described unrecognized and institutional racism in everyday life would be a routine story in an African American or Latino newspaper.[37]

Despite the news media's preoccupation with yuppies, soccer moms, free-spending baby boomers, and other upper-middle-class Americans, the largest number of Americans are working- and lower-middle-class people, even if the former prefer to think of themselves as "working people."[38] Although the news media cannot divide up their newsholes to represent each of the major population groups in their markets, they could be more representative.

If newspapers can report changes in the stock market for the investor, they can keep track of changing wages and benefits for workers. While they cover crime victims, journalists should report on the perpetrators as well, try to determine the causes and conditions that led to their crimes, and portray them as human beings gone wrong rather to identify them only by their crimes.

As always, the poor have the greatest need for news about the world they live in, and for news that respects them and their perspectives on the world. At present, most journalists are not aware of the kinds of news various kinds of poor people find useful. Need would suggest stories about available work at decent wages; crime-free areas with vacant housing; stores selling high-quality goods at low prices; and helpful services that are not punitive. Those still on welfare have to find out which welfare offices are useful in helping recipients obtain jobs, which clinics and emergency rooms supply the best medical care, and more generally, which agencies serving the poor humiliate them the least.

The fastest way to move toward a multiperspectival approach would be to add journalists from different socioeconomic backgrounds. Women have been able to enter the once all-male newsrooms and even break the glass ceilings that have restricted their upward mobility, but the newsroom class makeup, and therefore the racial one, remain sadly deficient. Good intentions are clearly not working and in the academy as in the newsrooms, new recruitment methods and criteria of merit must be invented to end discrimination against people of working-class origin and varied skin colors.[39]

As long as the news media write and tell the news in middle-class English, people who do not write using the mainstream language remain ineligible. The resulting style bind could be broken most easily on television, where on-camera talent speaking working-class or non-middle-class English might even boost the ratings.[40] The print media could hire non-middle-class reporters whose work could be rewritten by middle-class writers. They might even permit some deviations from "standard" English and see how they are received.

Like all other employers, the news media follow the conventional age biases, but if they could, for example, hire young people to investigate and report Washington political stories relevant to their peers, they would add a fresh perspective to inform adults and might even raise the number of young people in the news audience. Journalists from low-income backgrounds could report the society news, and foreign journalists from every country in the world with a free press would certainly supply new angles on American politics, and the business community. Opportunities for instructive deviations from standard journalism are humongous.[41]

More representative news media are also needed as badly as ever to serve the currently unserved. Free newspapers and radio programs edited by and for poor people still deserve to be tried. The internet has, as already noted by practically everybody, the greatest technological potential. Websites that deviate from standard journalism already exist, but most are controlled by amateur or professional ideologues. Professional news organizations are costly whatever the technology, and multiperspectival news sites are just as expensive as mainstream ones. Making them visible as economically and politically powerful news organizations take over the internet is also costly.[42]

Other News Formats

Times may change, but news media formats for straight news are amazingly stable. Most newspapers still consist of columns, with stories topped by headlines, important news at the front, and sports, comics, and lowbrow material at the back. The half-hour news has not departed significantly from the format it borrowed from half-hour radio news 40 years ago, and today's internet news strongly resembles a small news magazine or tabloid newspaper. Clicking on a link is not terribly different from turning a page.

Perhaps it is time to consider some changes. A number of television professionals have predicted that if the audience for the network evening news declines further, it may be turned into a five-to-eight minute introduction to a daily news magazine. On days with stories that require more time, one or more sectors of the news magazine could be co-opted for this purpose.[43] Actually, three network news programs are already heading in this direction; several days a week, national and international news takes up only a few minutes, while the rest of the time is taken up by political, medical, and other features.

But other possibilities might be explored as well. The significant number who watch the network news or their cable equivalents only once or twice a week might be better served with a weekly news program to recap the important stories for people who only watch once a week. There might even be room for a national weekly paper, a *USA This Week*, for people lacking the time or interest for a daily paper. Or else, *Time* and *Newsweek* would perform this role.

The costs of supplying the news in the event of permanent audience decline might be cut by increased pooling. Today's news media are so competitive that each wants to put its stamp on the same news story, even if the end result is often so similar that only professionals can spot the differences. This competition would be justified if more stories were actually covered differently, as they would be if multiperspectival news existed.

Involuntary pooling, which is sometimes required by the Pentagon and other official sources, is unacceptable, but voluntary pooling has long been acceptable as syndication, which supplies newspapers with the same stories and columns that appear elsewhere. Even the common use of the stories put out by the Associated Press and other wire services is a kind of pooling.[44]

News audiences would miss little if the same stories, say of state rituals and ceremonies, political photo opportunities, other scripted events, and even some battles, accidents, and disasters, appeared in competing news media. In fact, if all news media used the same descriptive news of scripted events, reporters might be freed to go behind the scenes. From what is now known about news media and other audiences, people come away with a variety of interpretations of the same content anyway. Thus, the news is never as uniform for the audience as it is for the journalists.

Pooling would enable smaller newspapers and stations to increase other kinds of news coverage and could also be a way of preventing further shrinkage of foreign news. It might even curtail the closing of newspapers and television news operations in small communities and prevent a single owner from determining a community's entire news diet.

News and Humor

More radical format changes might be considered as well. Some members of the news audience, and some journalists too, are turned off by the often didactic tone of the news, and the humorlessness that accompanies it.

Straight news does not always have to be informational cod liver oil, especially since most news media add light touches and political cartoons but keep them strictly separated from the news. But why not end some of the separation between straight news and humor and develop a format in which political cartoons, satire, and other commentary were connected with the news on which it comments. Political cartoons are frequently more biting than even the most critical editorial, but the cartoons would be more useful if they were regularly placed with and more directly tied to the news stories on which they comment—or if brief summaries of the news that inspired the cartoons were attached to them.[45] Combined commentary on both news and satire would add another level of depth to the news. If cartoonists could only write and columnists draw, they might even comment on each other's work directly.

Television's political humor needs to be connected with the news as well. It is now strictly separated and segregated: on late-night network talk shows, in occasional sitcoms, and on cable channels. Instead political satirists could appear right after the evening news at least once a week.[46] A regular slot adjacent to the news might even offer mass media-satirists some protection against censorship and job loss that they now experience from time to time.

Despite the fact that today's entertainment abounds with irony, satire has not yet been tried in mainstream news media. Young people are said to be more at home with satire than their elders, and if some of them actually get their news only or mainly from satiric programs, more of them might pay attention to straight news if it accompanied or followed the political satire.

News Fiction

"News fiction" is fiction about topics in the news, for example, the "Washington" novels associated with Allen Drury and Ward Just.[47] A current television equivalent is "The West Wing," the sitcom-soap opera about life in the Oval Office. Films about politics like "Mr. Smith Goes to Washington" and "The Candidate" have become classics.[48] Probably the largest amount of news fiction has been produced as television docudramas. These take the form of fictions about the historical past, the most famous probably being "Roots," or partly fictionalized documentaries about specific events from the White House's handling of the Bay of Pigs to famous murder trials.[49]

Because news fiction has generally been popular, audience research might show that they persuade some people to start paying attention to real news. Alternatively, they could provide more detail about news events to that part of the audience that does not watch documentaries, read news magazines, or read books about news events. Watching television entertainment and movies encourages some people to obtain more information on their subjects in the library. News fiction might send people to the news media, and a twenty-first century Charles Dickens would almost certainly be able to do so.[50]

Journalists worry when news becomes entertaining but news fiction is not primarily entertainment; it is fictional or partly fictional storytelling that sheds light on the institutions and activities that are covered as news.[51] News fiction is as old as the hills. It must have existed long before Homer started turning war news into historical drama.

News fiction is hardly perfect by news standards, for it frequently oversimplifies the real world for storytelling purposes. Furthermore it is not averse to offering facile or magical solutions to social and political problems.[52] In Hollywood, love sometimes resolves political problems as it resolves other types of problems. But the fact remains that news fiction will inform more people than a documentary about the same subject. The question is whether and how such fiction can be put to uses that will enhance journalism's goals.

For example, television's "The West Wing" has, for all its faults, acquainted its viewers with White House politics in ways that the news media do not. However, these viewers might learn even more if a White House correspondent commented on each installment immediately afterwards and explained what the show's writers got right and wrong.

Conversely, docudramas can then go beyond the news story, adding details about the public figures involved, and elaborating on the contexts and conditions of events and statements that have become newsworthy. Docudramas can also speculate about motives and causes when journalists cannot determine them and suggest as fiction what cannot be conclusively proved by investigative journalists.

If news fiction were explicitly labeled as such, fictional ingredients were identified clearly, and the fiction were set off unmistakably from the news, the risk that some people might confuse fiction with nonfiction should be avoidable.

New Tasks and New Journalists

Most news is gathered by "generalists," all-purpose reporters who cover so many different topics that they often lack the background knowledge—or the time to acquire it—to ask the most significant or telling questions of their sources.

When generalists do not suffice, the news media turn to beat reporters, who often obtain special training in the fields or subjects they cover.[53] Beats and their reporters are more costly than generalists, however, and news firms seeking to increase their profit margins have cut back on beats and on the bureaus out of which they work.[54]

Nevertheless, in the long run, the news media must increase the number of beats to cover a world that is continuously becoming more interdependent. In the process, new technical issues requiring new journalistic expertise will be generated. Concurrently, international economics and politics will grow in importance, with consequences for domestic economic and political news. For example, in a politically interdependent world, national political news will become more complicated than the tugs-of-war between the two major parties that have been the staple of the country's political reporting for so long.

In addition, the overall educational level of the news audience, as of the rest of the country, is rising. Its interest in the news may not be rising as quickly, but still, generalists will require more knowledge, and more beats will have to be created. They will also need more philosophical sophistication, for an interdependent world requires an understanding of other cultures, as well as the ability to tell their audience—and themselves—that American values and assumptions about reality are not universal.

Where and how to supply the necessary training? Journalism schools are the logical place, but they would also have to adapt. Education in journalistic practice that many students have already learned while editing college newspapers is unnecessary.[55] So is the attempt to give people who have to cover the news an academic research veneer.[56]

Instead, journalism students need practical training in intellectual and substantive fields, particularly economics and the other social sciences, and to sharpen their analytic and explanatory skills, so that they can fully understand the contexts in which the events and statements they cover are embedded.[57] Otherwise, journalism students will be replaced by liberal-arts graduates who can write for the news media.

Most journalism schools cannot supply the needed training, but can find it in the academic divisions of their colleges and universities. The journalism schools have to translate what the academic divisions teach into the kind of knowledge journalists need. The translation courses could be taught by professors and practitioners of journalism, supported by academics who have some knowledge of and respect for journalism. Bringing the academics into the journalism schools has other virtues, such as reducing the often-immense intellectual distance between academics and professionals so that they can take advantage of each other's distinctive skills.[58]

Once upon a time, reporters who received their initial training in city-hall politics could be quickly retrained for foreign news. But as American foreign policy and politics increasingly move into yet little-known regions, foreign reporters need to be area specialists. Otherwise, they run the danger of reporting only the news sources that can afford English-speaking propagandists.

Paying for Better News

My last proposal concerns money. Virtually all of the suggested changes in the news made over the years will raise costs, and the ones in this chapter are no different. If the news is as central to democracy as journalists argue, then more needs to be spent so that its impact is maximized. Would news firms provide the necessary budget, and would they be satisfied with the profits of other firms with the same kinds of risk? The average profit in American firms is 6 percent. But the print media are not satisfied with even twice that percentage, and local television news firms expect considerably more.

Capitalists and shareholders are not receptive to sermons about lower profits, however, and more effective forms of pressure to raise news budgets are needed. For example, could enough journalists buy enough stock in their firms to vote on behalf of their professional interests?[59] Or should all workers, and audience members or customers, be represented on the boards of all firms? Is it possible to hope that the Federal Communications Commission will one day be able to insist that the public interest, and one broadened to include the interests of journalists and news audiences, be translated into budget requirements for the news media?

Once upon a time, particularly after the quiz scandals of the late 1950s, the television networks used their news divisions to obtain status and to counter criticism of their entertainment programs. Publishers of popular books established prestige divisions that were required to earn only a nominal profit or none at all but in return provided intellectual and artistic respectability to the rest of the firm. This tradeoff declined as the news media and the publishing business hit hard times and were merged into larger corporations and conglomerates that seemed less interested in prestige.[60] Still, some independent firms and conglomerates continue to maintain prestige divisions. Would the big conglomerates that make unusually high profits be willing to treat their news operations as a prestige division, in exchange for the goodwill they might harvest in return?

Another possibility is respectable bribery: offering news firms some kind of tax write off or other public subsidy in return for putting limits on their profits, or better still, for investing additional funds in the news. Journalists feel strongly about avoiding public subsidies because they fear that political pressure and some kind of censorship will inevitably follow.

News firms have been less reluctant to take public money, but largely for the construction of new buildings, or more correctly, for agreeing to stay and keep jobs in the community in exchange for building subsidies. Perhaps some way could be found to tie such subsidies to higher budgets for the firm's news operations.

However, if communities can spend money to keep news firms from leaving, they could also spend money to attract them, using the same tax and other subsidies with which they attract other new industry. Single newspaper and television station towns might appropriate subsidies to encourage journalistic competition, or attract new news media because they are labor-intensive enterprises that will add jobs.

In fact, the provision of government funds to keep journalistic jobs in the community could be used as justification, if justification were needed, to revisit the general question of government support of the news media. Despite all the dangers and other downsides that the use of government monies spell for the freedom and autonomy of the news media, there are other dangers and downsides when the monies come from the private sector. News firms may pressure and censor journalists less often than government, but if news firms continue to seek higher profits and lay off journalists to do so, government funding might look more desirable, particularly if the barriers between church and state described in Chapter 2 could be fortified.

A final suggestion is the establishment of economically alternative news media that would not require normal profits. One possibility is the creation of additional national news media as utilities or other limited-profit enterprises. They should earn a steady or even a guaranteed rate of profit, but it would be lower than that of current news firms.

A related possibility might be to resort to nonprofit enterprises. Public television could be enabled to field full news organizations, and perhaps nonprofit print media are possible too. Government support for such enterprises can be justified if they reach audiences not reached by other news media.

Finally, there is the uncharted and therefore tempting frontier of the internet and other new technology of the future.[61] I have already expressed my suspicion, like others before me, that mainstream news firms that have dominated the print and electronic media will also dominate the internet. Websites conducted by one or a small number of journalists and editorialists may increase in number, but comprehensive news organizations that can provide alternatives to the mainstream firms cost money. They cannot flourish without the requisite audience need and demand, as well as advertisers or a lot of web users willing to pay for their internet news.

Possibilities of Change

Several of the preceding suggestions are already in place or being tried somewhere, and others may come to fruition in the future. But some are so idealistic that they are currently only subjects for discussions and debates. Moreover, suggestions are in the end merely words unless constituencies organize around them. In this instance, the future depends largely on the news audience and whether a sufficient number will ever want more political and economic news. This can most likely happen only if enough people need the government and other public and private institutions and firms on which journalists report.

Today this is hardly the case. People's perceived need for government seems small, as long as it maintains roads, schools, and other public facilities on which they depend and does not directly threaten the economic security and standard of living of large numbers. No wonder, then, that the public's need for news is met largely by news summaries much of the time.

People's need for government might rise sharply if the economy falters for a long enough period—or if new styles of life create a sufficient demand for additional government services. An increase in crime, terrorism, or other recurring threats to the social fabric might have a similar effect. Also, governments have been known to deal with crises or new popular demands without being responsive to the citizenry. If that were to happen, and if the news then spoke to people's concerns, the news audience might grow again, and on a more permanent basis.

Even under optimal conditions, the news can do little to persuade government to be more responsive to the citizenry. Other, more directly political measures would be required. Some of these measures are presented in the closing chapter.

CHAPTER 6

Citizens' Democracy: What Might Be Done

The news media and journalists can do little to reduce the political imbalance between citizens and the economic, political, and other organizations that dominate America. Very different policies and politics must be pursued to move the country toward what I called citizens' democracy in Chapter 1. Journalists could, however, play a role in several of them.

Toward Citizens' Democracy

Citizen's democracy is that form of representative government that maximizes the political responsibilities, rights, and most important, the public decision making of citizens without imparing the function of the economic and political system.

Citizens' democracy is not direct democracy, or the town-meeting governance of a small society. Nor is it an antidote to "political apathy," a notion that labels an impossible ideal a personal failing. Most people will remain political bystanders most of the time, and conventional citizen participation will remain the occasional activity it is today. The enlarged role of the citizenry would have to be implemented through some different and new institutions that are grounded in a greater degree of political equality, not only between citizens and organizations, but also among them.

Paths to Citizens' Democracy

In the rest of the book, I discuss a half-dozen ideas that might help move the country toward citizens' democracy.[1] Some are feasible or almost so, but most cannot be realized unless and until today's political inequalities are reduced.

This chapter is not meant to be a blueprint for action, however; it is, rather, an exercise, or the beginning of one, to figure out what citizens' democracy means and might require if it could be implemented in the future.

Journalists can play a role in this exercise too, by reporting ideas and suggestions for citizens' democracy. Now they limit themselves primarily to proposals for immediate action espoused by elected officials and occasionally experts. Stories about longer-range ideas should be newsworthy too, however, at least when news days are slow. If journalists can publicize yet-unachieved technology, they can also cover ideal political schemes.

The Proposals

Democratize Elections   Once new voting technology has been installed and the federal government enforces people's right to vote, attention should shift to nonvoters. Enabling and persuading both sporadic and regular nonvoters to show up at the ballot box would constitute one small step toward the reduction of political inequality. Inequality would be reduced further if all citizens were enabled to vote, felons and ex-felons included. A larger step would eliminate winner-takes-all voting wherever possible. A yet larger, though impossible step would reform the Senate so as to eliminate the unfair advantages of the small state and their residents.

People who need to be persuaded to vote probably need incentives, which will require a better understanding of why they do not vote and some rethinking of what people should be able to vote about.[2] Nonvoters might appear in the polling booth if they could cast a protest vote and indicate what they are protesting. Perhaps griping, which is probably the most popular form of public protest, could be institutionalized sufficiently to become a kind of protest voting, or a surrogate for it—and not just for current nonvoters. Some nonvoters might come if they could propose mandates for the candidates. If incentives could be found for elected officials to attend to some of the demands of nonvoters before elections, they might have reason to become voters. Even people who do not vote because they are content with the status quo need a chance to affirm their contentment, an affirmation that would surely be welcomed by incumbent politicians.

Concurrently, the news media need to correct their current lack of interest in potential and actual nonvoters. Fairness suggests that as long as half of the population does not vote, half the time and space given to reporting the presidential election campaigns should be devoted to nonvoters and people who are not sure they will vote.

Democratizing voting by attracting nonvoters is only half the battle, however. The other half is to democratize the supervision of elections. Perhaps a first step is to keep political parties and other political organizations away from the process, the polling booth, and the election-counting operation as much as possible, preventing their ability to bar voters who could threaten their power.

Preventing people from voting should be a punishable offense, and journalists can help with investigative reporting to identify the lawbreakers. Indeed, the news media should have undertaken investigative reporting in all the states of the union to determine whether the tactics used in Florida in the 2000 election were used in other states, and for how many past elections.

Democratization requires a reduction in the influence of the organizations that subsidize election campaigns and use it to gain extra lobbying advantage over elected officials. Although the more campaign finance reform the better, publicly mandated restructuring that requires corporations to maximize the welfare of workers and customers along with shareholders, executives, and directors would be far more desirable. Then corporate and other organizations' exertions of political pressure might be close to the interests of a larger number of citizens.

Despite its shortcomings, public funding of elections would somewhat reduce the imbalance between the citizenry and the organizations that will always send monies or other resources to campaigns, making a little more room for citizens' democracy. Public financing may not be feasible, however, until citizens trust government enough to allow it spend their taxes to elect public officials.[3]

The political parties have few incentives to cut back on campaign spending, but shortening formal election campaigns might help, particularly now that informal campaigning has become permanent.[4] If the shortened campaigns were dominated by various kinds of debates and candidate interview programs, expensive campaign advertising might be less necessary than it is now.[5]

The debates would require virtually no campaign expenditures other than the cost of radio and television time and its internet equivalent, and they as well as the interviews should be news carried as a public service performed by the television and internet companies.

Even if campaigns could be shortened or the traditional campaigns funded entirely by public monies, the flow of corporate and other money that provides political access would probably not stop. When organizations need government help to obtain contracts and tax breaks, they will find ways of helping the elected officials they need.[6] Maybe campaign contributions would be reduced somewhat if the contributors could no longer treat them as tax deductible costs of doing business, but preferential access to elected officials to obtain unfair advantages has to be discouraged in other ways as well.

Democratize Other Forms of Political Feedback   Voting remains the only citizen feedback for public officials that counts, but a number of other feedback mechanisms are available in a democracy. As I have suggested several times, most are more easily accessible to the highly educated, affluent, and thus easily organized citizens, making the equalization of feedback particularly urgent.[7]

Polling people is probably the most egalitarian of feedback methods, but it too can stand further democratization. Until the unlikely time when everyone votes, polling is more democratic than voting because properly drawn samples can represent the entire population. Pollsters also have a better chance of reaching habitual nonvoters, including even some of those fearful of any contact with the government.

True, pollsters report that 40 percent or fewer of the people contacted are willing to be interviewed, but the proportion voting is often no higher, and pollsters can weight responses to sample the entire population while the government cannot.[8]

Unlike elections and referenda, polls cannot be influenced by campaign donors. Instead, they are influenced by the questions they ask and their wording. In order for polling to be democratic, questions therefore have to come from several sources, and address topics and issues of priority to various sectors of the citizenry rather than those of the pollsters and the various users of their polls.[9] In addition, polls would have to be undertaken by a variety of organized and unorganized interests, including marginal groups whose ideas rarely appear in the public agenda.

Polling itself would have to be reformed, however. Among other things, questions need to be more specific and, when they concern public policies, framed to inform respondents of the financial and other costs of policy alternatives.[10] That major national political decisions and strategies are sometimes based on answers to one poll question: "Do you approve or disapprove of the way (name) is handling his job as president?" is beyond belief.

Even improved polls must, however, be complemented by in-depth interview studies that ask small samples more probing and less superficial questions than polls. Interviews would be especially useful, and far more so than focus groups, to understand people's concerns in the detail necessary for intelligent policymaking.[11] The news media should be eager to cover the results of interview studies; they supply richer answers than polls and can be reported in narrative styles. Thus, they make better stories than polling numbers.

Polls and interviews are also needed to represent downscale Americans as long as they vote less often than upscale citizens. As a supplement to voting, polling would enable the citizenry to demand changes in policies during the two years between elections, and the same polls could warn these officials that they must consider changes if they want to be reelected.

If polling could be democratized, ways of relating the results of voting and polling might be explored. For example, if national samples of poll respondents were asked many of the same questions asked voters at exit polls, pollsters could project electoral outcomes that assume everyone eligible had voted.[12] These projections would call attention to the differences between the voting and the actual populations, illustrate the indirect role played by nonvoters—and perhaps even persuade a few nonvoters to show up at the voting machines next time.

Add Citizen Lobbies   The goals of citizens' democracy notwithstanding, American politics will continue to be sufficiently dominated by large organizations, and citizens will have little choice but to get on the organizational bandwagon themselves. Consequently, they need to establish the citizen equivalents of the advocacy, pressure, and other groups that now represent the big organizations.

I think of these equivalents as citizen lobbies. A small but mounting number of such lobbies are already at work in Washington and elsewhere. As I pointed out in the first chapter, the organizations working for senior citizens and on environmental issues are often identified as citizen lobbies, but many other organizations also function as de facto lobbies. They include, for example, the constituent organizations of the many social movements that have emerged since the 1960s, democratic unions, as well as the formal groups that advocate or defend the interests of parents, patients, students, voters, and other sets of citizens.

Citizen lobbies obtain their power from the size of their membership or active supporters, the numbers whom they can mobilize on behalf of causes, legislation, and other activities, and the funds and information they can generate for supporting and "educating" public officials. Lobbies can also try to inform their members and supporters about under-the-radar and technical issues relevant to their interests. Then, when such issues appear on the political agenda, citizen lobbies can try make sure that "organized interests" are balanced by "citizen interests."

Nevertheless, more citizen lobbies are needed to represent citizens inside and outside the beltway. One lobby, needed for all the citizens on wages and salaries, is an employee lobby, which speaks for employees of various kinds and strata who cannot or do not wish to belong to unions.[13] If employee lobbies could develop even a portion of the political influence once exercised by unions, they could be particularly useful to the workers who now have few or no rights.

I use the term lobbies loosely, but they can be membership organizations or nonmembership ones that merely collect dues or contributions. Although some observers are critical of the latter for being run by hired hands, the structure of the organization is less important than the quality of advocacy and pressure the organization can supply.[14]

Moreover, while lobbies are traditionally seen as making demands on government, they can and should also lobby other large organizations, particularly economic ones. Citizens outside the consumer movement who are unhappy with consumer product design or quality, pricing policies, or other kinds of economic issues, have a right to make demands of and put pressure on private enterprise. Consumer goods industries are actually particularly vulnerable to lobbying because, as suggested in Chapter 4, they need to protect their goodwill.

Lobbies stand between the large society and individuals, much like the clubs and other voluntary associations so admired by Robert Putnam, and de Tocqueville and others before him. Voluntary associations rarely have been active in political matters, however. Conservatives have proposed "mediating structures," "points of light," and "faith-based" social services but these are intended to reduce government, not to put pressure on it.[15]

Other political activists have instead proposed "civil society," a multifaceted conception revived by the political associations that helped to overthrow Eastern Europe's Communist regimes. These associations, made up of activists, intellectuals, and professional politicians, later turned into political parties.[16] Such associations do not exist in America, for most organizations that are attached to public institutions, such as the Parents-Teachers Association or the League of Women Voters must remain officially nonpolitical even though they play a political role. Whatever the virtues of these organizations, they generally do not serve democratizing functions. Even if European-style civil society could be brought to the United States, there is no guarantee that it would represent citizens before and against government and the private sphere here. The American political system is just too different from European ones.

Lobbies lack the civic image and small-town symbolism associated with voluntary associations and civil society. In fact, lobbies are closer to unions than to other organizations open to ordinary citizens. Lobbies are more flexible than other associations and can carry out virtually any kind of organizational and political activity.[17] Moreover, citizens play many roles, in the family, on the job, as homeowners or tenants, in religious and secular organizations, among others, and each role can give rise to several interests. As consumers of many goods, citizens might need not only lobbies that deal with relevant retailers, but also those that rein in distributors and manufacturers. Citizens are users of many services; they are patients—as well as parents and children of patients—clients of various professionals, and participants in recreational and other organizations. They are also touched, directly or indirectly, by virtually every piece of legislation that comes up in Congress, in state and local legislatures, and other political bodies. They are often the intended beneficiaries of government regulators, and regulators that are pressured by lobbies of the regulated could use help from citizens. No single person has the time, money, dedication, or level of interest necessary to belong or even contribute to more than a handful of lobbies, and most people will never have any affiliation with a lobby, but the number of possible citizen lobbies is huge.

Partly because of the multiplicity of citizen roles, some citizen lobbies will be in direct conflict with each other. Even the dividing line between citizen and organizational lobbies could be a source of conflict, because the boundaries are not always easily drawn. Citizens are also members of corporate and other organizations in one or another of their roles; they may be tenants as well as landlords. As a result, people could be supporting both organizational and citizen lobbies concurrently, but then they can already belong to a number of incompatible groups. The chance that the number of such groups would increase drastically if lobbies proliferated is small.

Politics is messy, and democratic politics even more so, but messy democratic politics is much preferable to neat plutocracy. Because conflicting interests are abundant, citizen lobbies will compete with each other, make alliances with organizational lobbies against other citizen lobbies, or engage in internal factional disputes. When lobbies are large and members or supporters can be counted in the millions, they may have trouble coming up with a single position on a controversial issue.[18] Such problems are inevitable and to be expected, but they are less serious than the absence of sufficient citizen lobbies on the political battlefields.

Even when they are called citizen lobbies, they are often going to be run by specialized professionals, including lobbyists. As in other organizations, staffs have their own interests that at times conflict with those of the citizens paying their salaries.

A more serious shortcoming of citizen lobbies is that affluent and educated citizens will be better represented by lobbies than the rest of the citizenry. This shortcoming, another aspect of upscale democracy, could be partly compensated for by alliances of lobbies representing less affluent citizens. But upscale democracy will never completely stop raising its ugly head.

Congress and the federal bureaucracy may have no desire to deal with yet more lobbies, but they might encourage citizen lobbies, particularly those representing large numbers of voters. Private enterprise would probably be even less happy about being lobbied by citizens. Many have never learned to cope with dissatisfied but unorganized customers, or with the handful of organizations that now struggle against unsafe products, dishonest financial practices, and worker exploitation.

Lobbies are now so important in the country's political life that journalists ought to pay more attention to the ones that currently exist, treating them as the political organizations they are. The news media should be following participating lobbies closely when they participate in drafting, debating, marking up, and campaigning for legislation relevant to their clients' interests. Important stories can be found in their funding sources and their access to, "education" of, and persuasiveness with elected officials.

A sizeable number of investigative reporters could be kept busy with deceptive lobby practices alone. Given journalism's interest in citizen participation, journalists should be particularly interested in covering the several, and sometimes unsavory, kinds of "grassroots" citizen mobilization in which lobbies engage.[19]

The internal activities of lobbies are as newsworthy as those of other political bodies. For example, strategy debates and disputes, staff disagreements, relations with their employers and the people they lobby, lobby coalitions, and interlobby conflicts should be reported the same way as the internal squabbles and other dynamics of White House staffs, congressional committees, and political parties.[20]

The same coverage should be extended to citizen lobbies. These may still be small and few in number, but citizens should have information about what they do, and what they do badly. In some respects, citizen lobbies are at times more representative of citizen interests than elected officials, and thus deserve to be reported like other political bodies.

Lobbies have many faults, including lack of accountability, the possibility of co-optation and corruption, and unsavory practices. Indeed, political life would be quieter without lobbies of any kind, and a truly representative democracy would be preferable. However, the country is too big, too diverse, and too highly organized to do without lobbies.

Democratize the Economy   As now defined, citizenship is limited to people's political rights and responsibilities. However, the economy being more important to people's well-being and to their everyday existence than government, citizens should also have democratic citizenship rights and responsibilities in the economy.[21]

Three kinds of economic democracy are needed most urgently. One is literal, providing people with representation in the economic institutions that affect their lives. The specifics of representation need careful planning so that those represented obtain real benefits without impairing the health of the economy. Although a properly organized economic democracy should manifest higher employee morale and thus more productivity than a conventional economy, economic democracy that discourages the creation of jobs, incomes, and capital serves no one.

In theory, government is expected to protect the citizenry from at least the harshest effects produced by and through the economy. When the organizations that dominate the economy also play highly influential roles in government, however, elected officials are caught between organizations and citizens, with the citizens paying the costs in amount and quality of protection. Republican administrations are particularly quick to withdraw protections from the citizenry when they take over the White House, beginning with such basics as occupational safety, medical care, and consumer protection. As of June 2002, neither party was doing anything for the Enron and other workers who lost their jobs and retirement funds while executives were walking off with millions.

When interpreted literally, economic democracy requires that people who are direct or indirect participants in economic establishments be represented on the boards, committees, partnerships, and the like that run them. Whatever the establishments, manufacturers or service industries, wholesalers and retailers, professional offices, nonprofits, and even government agencies, their workers and customers or clients or patients need representation, as does the general public if and when it is not represented by elected officials.[22]

Adding layers of citizen representatives to economic and other establishments undoubtedly complicates their functioning, could reduce their efficiency, and would certainly interfere with the autonomy of the people who now control these establishments. Even the modicum of European "co-determination"—the workers' councils and unions that share decision making in the firms of some European countries—has been blamed for high rates of unemployment and weak economic growth although such codetermination exists also in countries with low unemployment and strong growth.

European unemployment may, however, be no higher than America's. For when this country's actual jobless rates are computed, they rival high European numbers. Adding involuntary part-timers, people who dropped out of the labor force because they could not find work, and others like them nearly doubles the official jobless rate. Meanwhile, the preoccupation with "efficiency" (read: profit maximization) ignores the human and other costs of the many American jobs that pay less than a living wage. Giant American corporations that must obtain the votes of its workers and other citizens would have to act somewhat differently in the economy and in the polity than today's giant corporations.

The second kind of economic democracy is the provision of some guarantee that every citizen, of the economy as well as the polity, has as much economic security as the country can deliver. Elected officials will and should be debating how much the country can deliver, but it should be enough to enable its members to be, and feel themselves to be, full members of American society and full citizens. Economic security entails full employment, or as much full employment as possible when jobs are scarce, while job security means a secure income that meets living-wage criteria, and welfare state services that by now are correlates of economic security.

Even if economic citizens are represented in economic institutions, these institutions are unlikely, if able, to guarantee optimal economic security. In other than a corporatist society, that guarantee falls to government. But the citizens who need that guarantee the most are likely to vote the least, for all the economic and other reasons cited in Chapter 1.[23]

The third form of economic democracy is the development of sufficient economic equality to enable every citizen to take advantage of the political opportunities and to obtain the political skills and rewards that now accrue mainly to people with high income and education. As the emergence of upscale democracy and the failures of the poor even to vote suggest, more economic equality is actually a prerequisite to political equality. Greater equality of wealth and incomes are not likely to be achieved soon, but a constitutional amendment spelling out an economic bill of rights would at least make it possible to legislate against the most extreme forms of economic inequality.

Democratize Government Itself Strange as it may sound, government, or parts of it, also need democratization. As I noted already, most citizens have most of their governmental contacts with bureaucracies, and the appointed officials responsible for them. Elected officials are supposed to represent their constituents but appointed officials are under no such compulsion. Beholden to the elected officials who appoint them or to civil service regulations, they can easily lose sight of their citizen constituents.

In theory it might be possible to elect citizen representatives to government offices, from the top-level ones that run agencies to the bottom- or street-level ones that serve the general citizenry. Aside from the conflict of interest between such citizens and the currently elected officials responsible for these bureaucracies, there is the question of how many candidates voters would be prepared to elect at every election.

Perhaps one solution is ombudspersons: an office responsible for ensuring that government agencies are user-friendly or otherwise responsive to the citizenry. Some of the staff of such an office would be located at the higher levels of government agencies, many more at the lower levels and the branch offices. They would also have some countervailing powers when bureaucratic staffs get too close to the powerful. The General Accounting Office is a federal agency that provides oversight of the government for the Congress; the ombudspersons would do that and more for the citizenry.

As in the case of the other organizations proposed in this chapter, the people responsible for adding citizen input to American democracy will be as imperfect as those we now elect. Some will be politicians or aspiring ones, others will represent already powerful constituencies, from party leaders to corporations, and some will be co-opted by those they are supposed to oversee for their fellow citizens.

Normal economic and political forces and processes continue to manifest themselves even when new functions are added to existing agencies. Some good ideas and good people will be overturned or corrupted, but many others will not be, and these others justify innovations, whatever their purpose. Power holders obtain their pound of flesh even from the most intelligent new policies, but that is no argument against such policies.

Rethink Democratic Theory Theory does not drive political or economic change but it plays a supporting role.[24] For that reason alone, democratic theory, or at least applied democratic theory, needs to be de-hellenized. Today's representative democracies cannot be inspired by the decision-making arrangements of the ruling aristocrats in a city-state that existed nearly 3,000 years ago.

Partly because of the increased power of conservative activists and thinkers, contemporary theorizing has become preoccupied with the responsibilities of citizens. Consequently, expanding the rights of citizens has not received much theoretical attention, and theorists need to ask what citizen rights should be guaranteed and strengthened in a polity dominated by big economic and other organizations.

Practically inclined theorists must attempt to figure out how far America can move toward a citizens' democracy, and with what consequences for the country, while those concerned with standards debate how far it should go in that direction. Elected representatives would probably find it harder to make decisions if citizens had to be consulted more often, but people would benefit from more access to and influence over these representatives.

Big societies may only be able to function if they are run by big organizations. In that case, the theorists must ask what effective political activities are left over for citizens. Because most people never participate actively in politics or civil society, maybe such activities would have to take place almost exclusively in big citizens' organizations.

The theorists also have to go one step further: to rethink citizenship and citizen roles, other than those spelled out in the Constitution. Setting aside such routine acts as obeying the laws of everyday life, most individuals act as citizens mainly if and when they vote or run for office. Meanwhile, citizenship ignores the social groups and institutions to which these individuals devote most of their time, energy, and emotion. As many have noted, a concept of citizenship based on equal treatment under the law mistreats those low in income and political influence.

Citizenship must be more than a term taught in civics courses; it ought to cover rights and responsibilities that pertain to important spheres of life other than the political and legal ones. But such a notion of citizenship and the society in which it can work still needs to be thought out.

Moving Toward Citizen's Democracy

I began this book by describing the popular belief—a part of the American Dream—that citizens are ultimately in charge of American democracy. The Dream remains the ideal it always was, but in everyday life, national politics and democracy are low in priority. Although a sizeable majority of Americans elected a slightly left of center presidential candidate in 2000, the president they wound up with came from the hard right and quickly, and at times autocratically, implemented hard-right policies—without visible objection from the citizenry at the time.

To be sure, Americans never paid much attention to ideology and Bush projected a less off-putting public persona than Gore. Moreover, many Bush voters also favored these policies. Nonetheless, the public passivity of the Gore supporters reflected once more the degree to which people are distanced from politics and see themselves as untouched by government.

In a country as big as America, few issues will ever grip a massive majority and few policies will obtain that level of support. Until economic and political conditions evoke widespread demand for the same policies, energize a sufficient number of previously quiescent citizens to relevant social movements, and appealing political entrepreneurs pressure more citizens, citizens' democracy will remain an ideal. It may always remain an ideal, but taking it seriously is nonetheless a worthwhile exercise.

NOTES

Chapter 1

1. Journalism has many other purposes; it reports for the nation and the "public," what they think or feel, including when no data on people's thoughts and feelings are available. Sometimes, the empirical and normative meld; then journalists also report what the nation and the public should feel. In disasters that are seen as national, journalists console the nation and the public, as well as express its actual, and its obligatory, patriotism.

2. Anthony Lewis, "Hail and Farewell," *New York Times*, 15 December 2001, A31.

3. Anthony Lewis, "Democracy and the Free Press: Are they Incompatible?" *Bulletin, the American Academy of Arts and Sciences* (March 1997): 49–63, quote on 62.

4. Quoted in William Kovach and Tom Rosenstiel, *The Elements of Journalism* (New York: Crown, 2001), 19.

5. The journalists' version of the Dream has a number of other shortcomings that will be discussed in Chapter 3.

6. John Quirt, *The Press and the World of Money* (Byron, Calif.: Anton/California Courier, 1993), 6. According to a *New York Times*-CBS News poll conducted just before the 1996 election, a third of those asked thought that it made no real difference who was elected president, up from 20 percent in November 1976.

7. James K. Galbraith, "Corporate Democracy: Civic Disrespect," *Dissent* (Spring 2001): 23–26, quote on 23.

8. Everett C. Ladd and Karlyn H. Bowman, *What's Wrong: A Survey of American Satisfaction and Complaint* (Washington, D.C.: AEI Press, 1998), 99. This poll asks which of the three "will be the biggest threat to the country in the future." Other polls ask the question differently, but almost always in terms of these three institutions, or metaphorical versions of them.

9. In fact, the unions are big mostly at election time, when many of them can still turn out the vote.

10. Bureau of the Census, *Statistical Abstract of the United States 1999* (Washington, D.C.: Superintendent of Documents, 1999), table 1299.

11. For a comprehensive and powerful statement, see William Greider, *Who Will Tell the People: The Betrayal of American Democracy* (New York: Simon & Schuster, 1992).

12. *Statistical Abstract*, 1999, table 891.

13. For a comprehensive study of low-wage workers, see Katherine S. Newman, *No Shame in My Game: The Working Poor in the Inner City* (New York: Knopf, 1999). For a more personal account, see Barbara Ehrenreich, *Nickel and Dimed: On (not) Getting By in Boom-Time America* (New York: Metropolitan Books, 2001).

14. Paul Krugman, "America the Polarized," *New York Times*, 4 January 2002, A21, citing Congressional Budget Office figures. The mean wealth of the top fifth of the population grew by 30 percent between 1983 and 1989; that of the bottom 40 percent declined by 76 percent. Edward N. Wolff, "Recent Trends in Wealth Ownership, 1983–1998," working paper #300, Jerome Levy Economic Institute, Bard College, April 2000, table 3.

15. See e.g., M. Harvey Brenner, "Political Economy and Health," in Benjamin C. Amick III et al., eds., *Society and Health* (New York: Oxford University Press, 1995), 211–246; Richard G. Wilkinson, *Unhealthy Societies: The Afflictions of Inequality* (London: Routledge, 1996); and Ichiro Kawachi et al., eds., *Income Inequality and Health* (New York: New Press, 1999).

16. I am indebted to Thelma Foote of the Center for Responsive Politics, who supplied me with these figures. (Personal communication, 14 December 2001).

17. The center estimated that the number of lobbyists increased by 13 percent between 1997 and 1999. According to "Washington's Lobbying Industry," a study prepared by the office of Rep. Dick Armey in June 1996, the number of lobbyists increased from nearly 17,000 in 1964 to over 67,000 in 1996.

18. Center for Responsive Politics, "Influence Inc.," (Washington, D.C.: The Center, 1998), 13, 18.

19. Ibid., 18.

20. Ibid.

21. The data were gathered from a sample of lobbies. Frank R. Baumgartner and Beth L. Leech, *Basic Interests: The Importance of Groups in Politics and Political Science* (Princeton: Princeton University Press, 1995), table 6–2.

22. Thanks in part to the diligent work of watchdog journalists, the access payments and their immediate purposes are no longer below the radar, but the negative consequences for consumers, workers, and fans of clean air may be years off and thus below the radar almost by definition.

23. In 1999, a number of these funders were complaining about being pressured and blackmailed by political fund-raising. Presumably, they had no political or economic reasons to contribute to election campaigns, but organizations or individuals who have reason to contribute are never in short supply.

24. At the time the U.S. Supreme Court awarded the 2000 presidential election to George W. Bush, the wife of Supreme Court Justice Clarence Thomas was being paid by the Heritage Foundation to identify and recruit conservative candidates for vacant federal judgeships.

25. Census data on voter turnout showed that lower- and moderate-income citizens voted far less often than—and sometimes at half the rate of—high-income ones. Bureau of the Census, "Voting and Registration in the Election of November 1996," (Washington, D.C.: Government Printing Office, 1997), Current Population Reports P20-504, table 12, 55. The data are based on reported voting. See also Ruy A. Teixeira, *The Disappearing American Voter* (Washington, D.C.: Brookings, 1992), chapter 3.

26. Robert W. McChesney, "Producer Power," *Boston Review* (Summer 2001): 18.

27. The pollsters do not even ask many questions about economic power holders, instead they concentrate so much on government that they might be evaluating it for the Government Accounting Office, as well as their own commercial and other clients.

28. I have also avoided questions tainted by a variety of other methodological problems, and indicated when findings could be affected by such problems. For example, when I believe question wording to shape answers, I quote all or the major parts of the questions for which I am reporting findings.

29. Pew Center, "Retropolitics," (Washington, D.C.: The Center, December 1999), 142.

30. Assent to this statement has risen from 45 percent in the mid-1960s to 72 percent in 1998. Center for Political Attitudes, "Expecting More Say," (Washington, D.C.: The Center, 1999), 20. That same year, 75 percent of those asked about the distribution of wealth agreed that "the rich are getting an increasingly larger share." Ibid., 21.

31. Ladd and Bowman, *What's Wrong*, 130–133. The figures for small business are almost three times as high as for big business, but small is almost always beautiful for poll respondents. Confidence in organized labor has always been lower than for big business. Ibid., 128.

    I should note that when several of the major pollsters ask the same or a similar question, Ladd and Bowman report the results of all the polls. For the sake of brevity alone, I have usually generalized the percentages across several polls.

32. Confidence in the White House however, has been low during the entire time these polls have been conducted. Ladd and Bowman, *What's Wrong*, 142. This is probably related to the general finding that confidence in institutional leadership is always lower than in the institutions themselves.

33. Seymour M. Lipset and William Schneider, *The Confidence Gap*, rev. ed. (Baltimore: Johns Hopkins University Press, 1983), 111.

34. For other analyses suggesting that the so-called trust questions actually deal with government responsiveness, see Teixeira, *The Disappearing American Voter*, 231; and Lawrence R. Jacobs and Robert Y. Shapiro, *Politicians Don't Pander: Political Manipulation and the Loss of Democratic Responsiveness* (Chicago: University of Chicago Press, 2000).

35. A number of other versions of the basic question are also used. Several can be found in Ladd and Bowman, *What's Wrong*, 83–86.

    I should note that almost all of the questions have a populist spin. Only big interests are not public minded, failing to benefit "all the people;" only politicians lose touch; and, only public officials are uninterested, or in the subsequent question, uncaring.

36. The question used for the longest period, from 1952 to the present, asks people to agree or disagree that "I don't think public officials care much about what people like me think." From 1952 to 1966, only a third of the respondents agreed with the statement, but the proportion rose to 50 percent during the 1970s and 1980s, climbed to approximately two-thirds early in the 1990s, and then came down slightly to 60 percent at the end of the decade. Ladd and Bowman, ibid., table 5–4, 83–84.

    The question has been asked by different polling organizations over the years, occasionally getting widely divergent responses the same year. Still, the overall trend has been the same, and most noteworthy, the positive response toward public officials during the prosperity in the 1990s came nowhere near what it was during the prosperity of the 1950s and 1960s. Most likely, popular disapproval of various political events and actions of that decade have played a role.

37. Henry Kaiser Foundation, "Government by the People: A Data Essay," *Public Perspective* (July/August 2001): 16–17. The poll was conducted by Princeton Research Survey Associates.

38. Pew Center, "Washington Leaders Wary of Public Opinion," news release, 17 April 1998, 6. Another study conducted a year earlier reports government officials hewing to a very different worldview than citizens. Two-thirds of the officials said that they were "satisfied with the way things were going in the world," but only a third of the citizens shared their opinion. Pew Center, "In Retrospect: Public Opinions 1997" (Washington, D.C.: The Center, 1998), 12. The Washington officials were congressional staffers. Another sample, of elites in business, news media, academia, and science, shared the staffers' contentment with the status quo.

39. Alexander Stille, "Suddenly, Americans Trust Uncle Sam," *New York Times*, 3 November 2001, A13.

40. Eighty-nine percent of respondents in a 1999 study agreed that congressional arguments about legislation were better explained as "point-scoring" than as "honest disagreements about policy." Center for Political Attitudes, "Expecting More Say," (Washington, D.C.: The Center, 1999), 6.

41. When respondents to another poll were asked to compare their own policy choices with those of elected officials, 80 percent agreed that "the nation would be better off" if "the leaders of the nation followed the views of the public more often." Center for Political Attitudes, "Expecting More Say," 10. Only 20 percent of the respondents thought the public was too "emotional, volatile and uninformed " to guide the government. Ibid., 12.

42. These observations are based on data in Ladd and Bowman, *What's Wrong*, chapter 6. See also Lipset and Schneider, *Confidence Gap*, chapter 2.

43. Since pollsters do not ask people why they feel as they do, it becomes difficult even to search for the reasons for the temporal, and other, patterns found in poll responses. For a careful analysis of the role of major political and other events, the economy, and other factors in explaining the poll results, see Lipset and Schneider, *Confidence Gap*, especially chapters 2–4.

44. The same general trend is reported in Robert D. Putnam, *Bowling Alone* (New York: Simon & Schuster, 2000), although he put most emphasis on showing a concurrent decline in associational activity, trust, and a catchall he calls "social capital," a technical term for what is commonly called "community" or "sense of community." Putnam also dates the downturn to the 1970s, but blames it on the absence of civic engagement and spirit among the baby boomers, and among other things, television that keeps people at home when they should be out in the community.

45. Another slight rise in positive responses was thought to be a reaction to the end of Republican attempts to drive Bill Clinton out of the White House.

46. Ladd and Bowman, *What's Wrong*, 79. A good statement of the historical pattern can be found in Schudson, *Good Citizen*, passim.

47. The differences between general and specific questions were first reported in Lloyd A. Free and Hadley Cantril, *The Political Beliefs of Americans* (New Brunswick: Rutgers University Press, 1967). See also Albert H. Cantril and Susan D. Cantril, *Reading Mixed Signals: Ambivalence in American Public Opinion about Government* (Washington, D.C.: Woodrow Wilson

Center Press, 1999). For general and specific responses about the federal government and individual agencies, see Pew Center, "Performance and Purpose: Constituents Rate Government Agencies," news release, 12 April 2000.

48. Pew Center, "Deconstructing Distrust," (Washington, D.C.: The Center, 1998), 16.

49. The study, which was conducted by the Pew Center, covered 20 news programs, and "60 Minutes." Pew Center, "Internet Sapping Broadcast News Audience," news release, 11 June 2000, 104–106.

50. These and related data can be found in David Whitman, *Optimism Gap* (New York: Walker, 1996).

51. Another mystery is the inaccurate belief in high and increasing rates of crime, teenage pregnancy, as well as the state of the deficit at a time in the mid-1990s when these were going down. Admittedly, the general public is not trained in statistics, and people's beliefs are affected more by events than numbers.

    Nevertheless, the empirically groundless negativism may have other causes, including the hostility expressed toward poor black people and toward the government respectively. The fear of crime may also be exacerbated—and justified—by the immense number of people (read poor black and Hispanic men) in prison. That people have always felt safe in their own neighborhoods can be read as whites, who are the majority of poll respondents, still live in mostly white areas where they encounter few of the young black males, particularly low income ones, whom they consider the cause of their fear of crime.

52. Pew Center, "Deconstructing Distrust," 130–134. Questions about trust and distrust of economic institutions were not asked. Other data, many based on American questions or roughly similar ones, reported from European countries as well as Canada and Japan indicate the same pattern of increasingly negative feelings about government and politics. Susan J. Pharr and Robert D. Putnam, "Why is Democracy More Popular than Democracies," *Chronicle of Higher Education*, 2 May 2000, B4–5.

53. Government waste is a popular journalistic topic, but journalists have not taken much interest in business wastefulness.

Chapter 2

1. Pew Center, "Internet Sapping Broadcast News Audience," news release, 11 June 2000, 24.

2. I am grateful to Jo LaVerde of Nielsen Media Research for these data.

3. Jim Rutenberg, "Audience for Cable News Grows," *New York Times*, 25 March 2002, C8.

4. Bill Carter, "CNN Returns to Its Element But Faces High Expectations," *New York Times*, 19 September 2001, C2.

5. In March 2002, the cable news audience totalled about one million viewers. Rutenberg, op.cit. The largest increase after 9/11 was reported by the Fox News Channel, which broadcasts a mixture of politically conservative and nationalistically slanted news and even more conservative talk shows.

6. At the start of the twentieth century, 99 percent of the country's daily newspapers were individually owned; by the mid-1980s, more than 70 percent were part of a chain. Daniel Bell, "Who Owns the Media?" *Correspondence* no. 6 (Spring-Summer 2000): 8.

7. This is an old American practice in other industries, notably the automobile industry, in which Ford, General Motors, and in the past Chrysler, have each always built several competing brands.

For a comprehensive analysis of these changes in the news media, see Ben H. Bagdikian's now-classic *Media Monopoly*, 6th ed. (Boston: Beacon, 2000); Robert W. McChesney, *Rich Media, Poor Democracy* (Urbana-Champaign: University of Illinois Press, 1999); also Bill Kovach and Tom Rosenstiel, *Elements of Journalism* (New York: Crown Publishers, 2001). In book publishing, the same process has progressed further, with a handful of giant corporations now controlling a large share of the international book market. See e.g., Andre Schiffrin, *The Business of Books* (London: Verso, 2000).

8. However, Time Inc. now publishes so many magazines that it has several magazine divisions and no single editor-in-chief can supervise them all.

9. A. J. Liebling, *The Press*, 2nd rev. ed. (New York: Pantheon, 1975), 32. Liebling was also prescient enough in the 1940s to warn journalists about the dangers of corporate ownership.

10. The subject of news media profits comes up rarely either in the professional or scholarly literature on the news media—and even among the critics of conglomerate incursions into the news media.

11. An analysis by the *Columbia Journalism Review* reports that the newspaper industry's average operating margin rose from 14.8 percent in 1990 to 21.5 percent in 2000. David Laventhol et al., "Profit Pressures: A Question of Margin," *Columbia Journalism Review* (May/June 2001): 18–25. A study of 13 major newspaper chains by the *American Journalism Review* reported that for 2000, their average operating profit margin was 22.7 percent. Alicia C. Shepard, "Moguls' Millions," *American Journalism Review* (July/August 2001): 21. These margins have declined between 2000 and 2002.

12. See, e.g., Shepard, "Moguls' Millions," 20–25. Curiously enough, journalistic critics seem more upset by celebrity journalists and their $50,000 lecture fees than by the $5 million that some top executives take home annually.

13. CNN has filled the foreign news gap left by the network news programs, but CNN is a cable TV channel and its audience is far smaller than those of the network programs.

14. The temporary visitors are called parachutists by the domestic journalists and the stringers who cover the news regularly for their country but sometimes also supply stories to American news media. Mark Pedelty, *War Stories; The Culture of Foreign Correspondents* (New York: Routledge, 1995).

15. Pew Center, "Self Censorship: How Often," news release, 30 April 2000. The figures for interference on grounds of advertising concerns are even more optimistic; 76 percent of national and 65 percent of local journalists report that advertising concerns do not influence news judgment very much or at all.

These figures invite questions about whether people responded accurately, though the questions asked for opinions, not assessments of respondents' own news organizations. Also, there is the normative question of how much is not much. Nine percent of the national journalists and 13 percent of the local ones thought corporate owners had "a great deal" of influence. The respondents included both executives and journalists, and some executives saw more corporate influence than the journalists, while others saw less.

16. Actually, news judgment includes some built-in audience considerations that enables the journalists to attract the largest possible audience for the news and for their work, and also makes money for the news firm.

17. For a thoughtful discussion of the pros and cons of conglomerate ownership of the news media, see James Curran, "Global media concentration: shifting the argument," www.open-Democracy.net, 22 May 2002. Open Democracy is a British online journal of opinion and the Curran article recaps a debate over the ownership issue that began in the journal in the fall of 2001.

18. Many journalists are too young to remember the owner tyrants of the past such as William Randolph Hearst, or Col. Robert McCormick, who ran the *Chicago Tribune* as an ultra-conservative newspaper for decades. In Chicago, he was sometimes described as "one of the finest minds of the thirteenth century."

19. Like their predecessor owners, the conglomerates are to some extent trapped. If they do not let the journalists report conglomerate troubles or if they limit the reportage to publicity handouts, the journalists (and the conglomerate) lose credibility. Concurrently, competing news firms will be sure to report, perhaps in more detail, the conglomerate's troubles and the censorship pressure, if any, it has exerted on its journalists. As in other professions, journalists protect each other.

20. A recent study of a nonrandom sample of journalists at national and big city news organizations reported a median income of just above $100,000, with 5 percent of the journalists earning under $50,000 and 14 percent $200,000 or more. The study asked for household rather than individual income however. See pamphlet by David Croteau, "Examining the 'Liberal Media' Claim" (New York: FAIR, 1998), 22.

21. Why such news is hard, and the rest soft, is an interesting question that may be better left to psychoanalysis. Social scientists make the same distinction, between hard and soft data, and scientists generally talk about hard and soft science.

22. See pamphlet by Thomas E. Patterson, "Doing Well and Doing Good: How Soft News and Critical Journalism Are Shrinking the News Audience and Weakening Democracy—and What News Outlets Can Do About It" (Cambridge, Mass.: Joan Shorenstein Center, December 2000). According to Patterson, critical journalism is literally more critical, "find(ing) fault with most everything that politicians say and do" (ibid., 9–10).

23. Some observers of television news believe that in the long run, the regular half-hour network evening news program will be replaced by daily news magazines that begin with five-to-eight-minute summaries of the day's domestic and international news. The evening PBS news program already follows this format, although its longer pieces are generally more detailed stories about particular domestic and foreign events or issues. The network evening news programs have informally adopted this format as well, except that the day's national and international news are not explicitly set off from the rest of the program.

24. The mainstream news media pay close attention to cable news programs, because if they dig up stories that attract unusually large audiences, at least by cable standards, the mainstream journalists will begin to cover these stories as well.

25. By mid-November 2001, over half the respondents of a Pew Center study said cable news was their main source of news, while only 18 percent said this about network news and 17 percent about local news. Pew Center, "Terror Coverage Boosts News Media's Image," news release, 28 November 2001, 3. Whether people meant that they turned more often to the all-day news channels than the basic ones that report the news only at prescheduled times,

or whether the viewers felt that they depended more on what they saw on cable than on the basic channels, is not clear.

26. In a very real sense, the evening news programs become the equivalent of the first paragraphs of a news story that runs on page one of the newspaper, the cable news programs supplying the detail of the remaining paragraphs that run on the inside pages of the newspaper.

27. The scandal coverage actually began with "tabloid television," television equivalents of the celebrity scandals featured in supermarket tabloids. The programs provided jobs for journalists but no hard news, and while they lasted only a few years, they legitimated the arrival of nonpolitical scandal coverage on mainstream television.

28. One story controversial enough to obtain more than a couple of days of coverage was the shootings at Columbine High School, which justified inquiries into and debates over gun control, as well as media violence in, and adult control over, the lives of teenagers to celebrity tragedies. The deaths of John F. Kennedy Jr. and his family justified discussions of airline safety; Hillary Clinton's candidacy as junior senator from New York sparked discussion on whether the First Lady should be allowed to stand for election. That one also provided room for discussions of Hillary Clinton's alleged virtues and vices.

29. One wonders how the cable news channels would have handled the Watergate story, which ran for two years off and on.

30. Now the internet enables the major news media (and others) to provide the very latest news, including scoops—as well as brief but expandable news summaries for what appears to be a drop-in audience still dominated by young people. At the same time, more and more news media reproduce their print and electronic news on their websites. Putting a newspaper on the web is of course cheaper than printing or delivering it.

31. The chart is reported in "Data Bank," *Brill's Content* (Fall 2001): 42.

32. Felicity Barringer, "Growing Audience is Turning to Established News Media OnLine," *New York Times*, 27 August 2001, C1, 6.

33. Perhaps these can always be downloaded into hard copy, although Reuven Frank has suggested (personal communication) that the 1930s scheme to manufacture television sets that could deliver print versions was found to be unfeasible because of the high price of the paper.

34. Pew Center, "TV Viewership Declines," news release, 13 May 1996, 64. The 1965 figure came from a Gallup study. For example, circulations and ratings rise during wars and decisive events like Watergate, the first O. J. Simpson trial, and Bill Clinton's impeachment. The figure for 2000 comes from Pew Center, "Internet Sapping Broadcast News Audience," 33

35. Pew Center, "Internet Sapping Broadcast News Audience," 75. Yesterday's radio news listening decreased from 58 percent in 1965 to 42 percent in 1995, but respondents may not have included car radio use (ibid., 65). For a more general analysis of the audience problems of network news, see Paul Farhi, "Nightly News Blues," *American Journalism Review* (June 2001): 33–37.

36. Pew Center, "Internet Sapping Broadcast News Audience," 23. In 1998, 56 percent agreed (ibid).

37. Pew Center, "Internet News Takes Off," 62.

38. Pew Center, "Public's News Habits Little Changed by September 11," survey reports, 9 June 2002, section I,2.

39. In the last quarter century, the audience for entertainment television has declined proportionally more than the television news audience.

40. So far, the trend has held up; the median age of the evening network news audience has hovered around 55 for at least the last quarter century.

41. The Society's concern with credibility has led to two studies: MORI Research, Inc., "Newspaper Credibility: Building Reader Trust" (Reston, Va.: ASNE, 1985). The second study was Christiane D. Urban, "Why Newspaper Credibility Has Been Dropping" (Sharon, Mass.: Urban and Associates, December 1998).

42. In 1966, 29 percent of the respondents had a great deal of confidence in the news media; this dropped to 14 percent by 1998. Confidence in TV news was initially lower than for the print news media but did not decline significantly between 1966 and 1998. The press was not the only institution to crash; confidence in law firms, for example, not declined by 100 percent during that period. Everett C. Ladd and Karlyn H. Bowman, *What's Wrong: A Survey of American Satisfaction and Complaint*, (Washington, D.C.: AEI Press), chapter 6, passim. According to one ASNE informant, the 1985 Credibility study was undertaken in response to similar confidence declines reported in Gallup polls between 1979 and 1983.

43. "The Press and the People: A Survey," *Fortune*, August 1939, 70; and Urban "Newspaper Credibility," table 3. The main complaints in 1998 concerned mistakes in spelling and grammar, although over 60 percent of the respondents indicated they felt better if the newspapers involved printed corrections.

    News audiences appear to be less concerned about inaccuracy in national news, in part because they are unfamiliar with details of the stories being reported, and partly because they are not interested in the small facts about public figures they consider important when the figures are local and private ones.

44. Factual inaccuracy is sometimes thought to be caused by bias as well.

45. MORI, "Newspaper Credibility," 18. This response may be another case of conflict and disagreement reducing people's confidence and trust, in journalists as in public officials.

46. "The Press and the People: A Survey," *Fortune*, 64–78.

47. MORI, "Newspaper Credibility," 16. "The average person," "senior citizens," "housewives", and "young people" led the list of those not covered sufficiently favorably (ibid, 36).

48. In 1998, 79 percent believed that the news media were responsive to people who were 40 to get into or stay out of the news, the top villains continuing to be public officials, elected and appointed, as well as "big business" and "wealthy people." Urban, "Why Newspaper Credibility Has Been Dropping," 8, tables 17-18 respectively. For another study suggesting increased journalistic unresponsiveness, see Pew Center, "Big Doubts about News Media Values," news release, 21 February 1999.

49. Pew Center, "Striking the Balance," 80. Unfortunately, the pollsters do not ask people what they mean by democracy, and exactly what the journalists fail to care about.

50. The same Pew Center study also reported that two-thirds of respondents agree that "journalists don't care about the people they report on." In 1985, half felt this way. Pew Center, "Striking the Balance" (Washington, D.C.: The Center, 1999), 80.

51. Seventy-five percent of respondents in the 1998 ASNE survey opposed reporting a family tragedy to respect the family's wish for privacy. Urban, "Why Newspaper Credibility is Dropping," table 30. However, only a third of respondents to the earlier ASNE survey said that their newspaper, and 40 percent, that TV News, "invades the average person's privacy"

(MORI, "Newspaper Credibility," 17). The question did not distinguish between local and network news.

52. Eighty percent of ASNE's 1998 survey respondents approved such reporting of corruption and other wrongdoing (Urban, "Newspaper Credibility," table 29). Two-thirds of respondents approved ABC television's use of hidden cameras to report a supermarket's selling of spoiled meat (Media Studies Center, "MSC Poll Finds Public Sympathetic to ABC in Food Lion Case," news release, 12 February 1997).

53. MORI, "Newspaper Credibility," 21, 23.

54. Thus, respondents unhappy with the news media in general were satisfied with their own daily newspapers. Unfortunately, no one has yet sought to ask the same question in both general and specific wording.

55. In fact it is entirely possible that if people need the news, they will feel more kindly about the news media; a frequent reward for the messenger with desirable news.

56. Pew Center, "Striking the Balance," 58, 74. This study also reports other professional self-criticisms.

57. Pew Center, "Striking the Balance," 58, 74, 75. The journalists are probably projecting their own overload reactions on their audiences, most of whom have more limited interest in the news than journalists, and are most likely also better at ignoring (and deleting) information that does not interest them.

58. Most likely, journalists do not think of themselves as having or lacking power, except perhaps in fighting the bean counters.

59. Conferences and journalism schools tend to invite well-known national figures that can attract large audiences, and local journalists rarely get chances to act as critics, except perhaps at professional conferences.

60. The primary Left critic is FAIR (Fairness & Accuracy in Reporting) that comments mainly on the conservative dominance of the news media and the role of corporate control in it. It also keeps track of media cave ins to advertisers and has done some useful empirical research on, among other things, what kinds of guests are chosen for television network panels and who is left out.

The most prominent Right critic, is AIM (Accuracy in Media), sees no corporate influences on the media and instead blames liberals, both for what appears in the news and for problems in the profession.

The internet has also spawned, or made room for, a number of organizations supplying "inside" news about the media, as well as commentary, some intentionally, more unintentionally ideological.

61. Kovach and Rosenstiel put it graphically: " . . . the news is increasingly produced by companies outside journalism. . . . We are facing the possibility that independent news will be replaced by self-interested commercialism posing as news" (*Elements of Journalism*, 13).

Interestingly enough, the journalistic rank and file may be less concerned than the leadership. The evidence is thin, but a Pew Center poll reports 26 percent of national and 37 percent of local journalistic respondents agreeing that corporate owners influence news organization news judgments a great deal or a fair amount (Pew Center, "Striking the Balance," 65). A third of the respondents saw news organizations declining in influence, but the study did not indicate what kind of influence was declining over what or whom (ibid., 80).

62. Like the rest of us, journalists are not consistent as they are as critical of big news corporations run by journalists as of others.

63. These have appeared in *The Columbia Journalism Review* and *The American Journalism Review*.

64. Reported in Pew Center, "Striking the Balance," and discussed also in Kovach and Rosenstiel, *Elements of Journalism*.

65. Whether simple yes-no, agree-disagree statements about journalistic values—and so stated that the professionally proper response was unmistakable—could be taken as an indicator of the respondents' adherence to these values is another matter.

66. Public journalism was originally "invented" by journalist "Buzz" Merritt and journalism professor Jay Rosen, but some of the projects have gone far beyond, or diverged considerably, from what its inventors had in mind. Davis B. Merritt, *Public Journalism and Public Life* (Mahwah, N.J.: Lawrence Erlbaum Associates, 1995); and Jay Rosen, *Getting the Connections Right: Public Journalism and the Troubles in the Press* (New York: Twentieth Century Fund, 1996).

67. One of the problems of public journalism is that most of the reports about its activities come from its supporters, advocates, and promoters. Not enough empirical work has so far been done to determine what works, when, where, and why, as well as what unintended consequences have occurred.

68. Of the many discussions of "infotainment," see e.g., Richard Reeves, *What the People Know: Freedom and the Press* (Cambridge: Harvard University Press, 1998), chapter 6. See also Neil Postman, *Amusing Ourselves to Death* (New York: Viking Penguin, 1985).

69. Indeed, journalists work hard to evoke such reactions—and yet others—in covering national disasters, from the Kennedy assassinations, to the explosion of the *Challenger* space craft and the bombing of the World Trade Center and the Pentagon.

70. The Simpson stories probably reinforced racial hatred and racial cohesion, but these too are not entertainment.

71. For examples of such critiques, see James Fallows, *Breaking the News* (New York: Pantheon, 1996), chapter 3; and Marvin Kalb, "The Rise of the 'New News'" (Cambridge, Mass.: Joan Shorenstein Center: Press, Politics, and Public Policy), discussion paper D-34, October 1998. For related, but more analytic, observations on journalistic self-criticism, see Michael Schudson, "Why the Informed Citizen is Too Much to Ask—and Not Enough" (Washington, D.C.: Pew Center for Civic Journalism, 1999), 4–14.

72. James Fallows is responsible for the term and the initial statement of the critique. Fallows, *Breaking News*, chapter 3.

73. The celebrity journalist now has peers in many other institutions, including even national research universities. If they are major audience magnets, even the highest-paid celebrities earn a small enough proportion of the total cost of doing business to make them a cheap method for increasing the number of customers. Paying a star $20 million to act in a movie is a bargain if he or she can add $50 million to its receipts.

74. This belief reflects journalism's logical positivism, and thus its attempt to make thought or research independent of the thinker or researcher.

    Ironically, there is even some practical truth to this belief. Although most celebrity journalists are thoroughly professional journalists, and would like to practice their craft, they frequently draw more attention than the people on whom they are reporting sometimes making it impossible for them to carry out reporting duties.

75. A number of national journalists have the opportunity to associate with important public figures, but they know that the opportunity is a function of their role. Celebrity journalists are able to associate and socialize with other celebrities, including the most important public figures, but no one has yet studied whether and how their view of America, and their overall news judgment are affected.

76. None so far earn the tens of millions earned by Hollywood movie stars and professional athletes. Even the honoraria are reasonably modest in comparison to those earned by some ex-presidents and other very visible politicians. They rarely exceed $40,000 or $50,000 per talk, but that is a huge sum in a profession in which many do not earn much more than that per year.

77. Some newspapers and other news organizations now forbid all outside speech making. A few working journalists have time to write books as well, but they rarely earn significant enough acclaim or royalties to join the list of celebrities.

78. Pew Center, "Striking the Balance," 59–60. The study did not ask the journalists' opinions of celebrity colleagues, however.

79. The image also comes in a politicized version in which the journalist is a fellow proletarian. It remains popular among some of today's journalists, and the ideologically driven critics of the Left and the Right. Indeed, the conservative belief in the journalist as a liberal and leftist menace may have originated in the proletarian image. There is also a little truth to the image, because some well-known journalists were Communists, although usually the Right considers journalists to be subversive because a large number vote democratic. That the Democrats are a majority party, and that most employed professionals also tend to vote democratic is ignored by the conservative critics—almost all of whom are funded by foundations allied with the Republican party.

80. Conversely, a handful of national journalists on elite newspapers came from upper- or upper-middle-class homes.

81. Norma Green, Stephen Lacy, and Jean Folkerts, "Chicago Newspapermen at the Turn of the Century: Bohemians All?" *Journalism Quarterly* 66, no. 4 (1989): 813–821, quote on 816. The article concludes that only a few were Bohemians.

82. Even the "proletarian" journalists of the 1930s seem to have been mostly middle-class people, and some were of considerably higher status.

83. John W. C. Johnstone, Edward J. Slawksi, and William W. Bowman, *News People: A Sociological Portrait of Journalists and their Work* (Urbana, Ill.: University of Illinois Press, 1976), table 2–10.

84. Ibid., table 3-1. By 1982, the college-educated proportion had risen to 80 percent. David H. Weaver and G. Cleveland Wilhoit, *The American Journalist: A Portrait of U.S. News People and Their Work* (Bloomington, Ind.: University of Indiana Press, 1986).

85. Closeness is difficult to measure, but historians of journalism could nevertheless study its past, and sociologists, its present.

86. I first heard this phrase from the sociologist Larry McGill when he was on the staff of the Media Studies Center. It can also be found in Richard A. Posner, *Public Intellectuals: A Study in Decline* (Cambridge: Harvard University Press, 2002).

87. Journalists also share the country's nostalgia for its real and imagined pre-urban past, and a journalistic pastoral could be constructed fairly easily.

88. Although radio had many of the virtues of television, it never had the status and

visibility of the print media and virtually became invisible after the arrival of television news.

89. So did the hour-long documentaries, which were expected to win prizes and gain prestige for the networks. Even so, they were usually scheduled against the competing networks' most highly rated entertainment programs.

90. Herbert J. Gans, *Deciding What's News* (New York: Pantheon, 1979), 222, 224

91. The contemporary perceptions of the 1960s and 1970s can be found in the autobiographies and memoirs of leading journalists of the time, such as Reuven Frank, *Out of Thin Air; The Brief Wonderful Life of Network News* (New York: Simon & Schuster, 1991); Leslie Midgely, *How Many Words Do you Want: An Insider's Story of Print and Television Journalism* (Secaucus, N.J.: Carol Publishing Group, 1989); and the many books about the *New York Times* and other newspapers of that period.

92. See e.g., James Fallows, "Internet Illusions," *New York Review of Books*, 10 November 2000, 28–31. Journalists have been fascinated with new technology before. Radio, for example, was widely expected to become a mass educational institution that would compensate for the shortcomings of the print media and the schools, and some journalists, such as Ed Murrow, expressed the same hope for television.

   The hope quickly turned to fear, however, for print journalists feared that the arrival of television news would mean the death, not only of radio, but all the print media as well. In fact, journalistic as well as other declinists thought television would also result in the death of conversation.

93. The profession's love affair with new technology is stimulated by technological determinism: the theory that technology itself can determine social institutions and human behavior. Determinists give too little thought, however, to the fact that most inventions disappear without a trace, and those that survive do so because there is government money to perfect them, because they fill some social needs, and are designed to fill these needs, including the need for profit. Primitive computers were first invented in the nineteenth century, but more than a century passed before the right designs coincided with the social needs for data and organizations' needs for labor-saving machines that could replace wage-earning humans.

94. To be sure, the internet also evokes fears among journalists, notably about people's ability to produce their own news stories, or to choose only the stories they want from the total stock of what is available. Both possibilities reduce the ability of journalists to determine the public's news consumption and could reduce the need for journalists per se.

95. Robert Putnam, *Bowling Alone* (New York: Simon & Schuster, 2000). I judge the journalists' excitement with his work by the frequency with which the book was reviewed and is still being referred to.

96. I ran a Nexis analysis for both books by titles only, in the major newspapers and magazine and journal sections, and during the year of publication and the next. (Wilson's book was published by Knopf in 1996.) I chose Wilson not only because he is often quoted in the press, but also because his book was, like Putnam, published by a major commercial publisher. During the year of and after the publication of his book, Wilson's book received 29 mentions in major newspapers, magazines, and journals, while Putnam's was mentioned 82 times.

97. The journalists' enthusiasm for Putnam's work was enhanced by his blaming the decline in

civic engagement on one of journalism's favorite villains, entertainment television. Even TV's journalists were more than ready to buy that one. Putnam's golden-age nostalgia may have been reflected in the discovery of the "greatest generation," the generation whose altruism and civic engagement helped win World War II. Tom Brokaw, *The Greatest Generation* (New York: Random House, 1998).

98. In fact, Putnam published an article with that title in *The American Prospect*, 11 February 2002, 20−22. He had, however, viewed wars as sources of social cohesion in *Bowling Alone*. For this analysis see Posner, *Public Intellectuals*, 314−315.

99. For example, although James Fallows is one of the most thoughtful analysts and critics of his profession, the last chapter of his book makes virtually no recommendations other than an endorsement of public journalism. James Fallows, *Breaking the News*, chapter 6.

I must note here that sociologists are not exactly active in or skilled at finding solutions to the problems of their discipline.

Chapter 3

1. It may thus be no accident that television anchorpersons sit on a dais when they dispense the news.

2. The court is reported as a body, mainly because all members are equal to the chief justice in writing decisions, the decisions are more newsworthy than the justices, and the justices are not available to reporters.

3. Important HUD news is reported from the White House, but then it claims credit for all federal accomplishments. Other HUD actions are apt to be ignored, in part because the agency is among the least powerful in the cabinet. This is common knowledge inside the beltway and among reporters, but the news audience does not know it and may never hear about these actions. Minor agencies, HUD included, become newsworthy when corruption and other dramatic activities are uncovered.

4. Columnists, commentators, and radio and television talk-show talkers may now accuse high officials of lying.

5. I borrow the phrase from Robert Entman, "The American Media and Race Relations in an Interdependent World" (Cambridge, Mass.: Joan Shorenstein Center: Press, Politics, and Public Policy, 28 June 2001), 2.

6. These processes are enhanced in wartime, when the president becomes commander in chief. Moreover, from the beginning of his administration, Bush's White House made sure that every positive governmental decision, even those that were routine, was attributed to the president. The White House sought to make Bush more presidential, but many journalists just reported the information from the White House and thus further legitimated a president whom future history may describe as the winner of a stolen election.

7. Admittedly, the journalists were in a bind, because they could not have called him the unelected president, or the president whose election remained controversial without causing a major outcry.

8. The journalists were not the only ones in a hurry, of course, for they were being pressured by the Republicans who were in the greatest rush. Even the general public may have added to the pressure, as many people, particularly those who were not enamored of either candidate, were ready for an end to the conflict.

9. Of course, incumbency creates its own kind of conservatism, because whatever ideology is in power, its advocates do not want a change in the status quo.

A contrasting view sees the conservatism of the news built into the news media themselves, particularly television; see Jeffrey Scheuer, *The Soundbite Society: Television and the American Mind* (New York: Four Walls and Eight Windows, 1999). Scheuer's analysis covers television in general, focusing mainly on entertainment television, but his notion that television's simplicity leads structurally and thus inherently to conservative fare is intriguing. Whether his hypothesis applies to news is another question, for news sources, journalists, and news firm executives and owners can spin the news to fit their ideological inclinations, at least to some extent. Moreover, exposes have inherently reformist subtexts, and are thus hardly conservative, at least as the term is commonly used. In social democratic countries, television news, at least the news on public television stations has a social democratic spin. The medium itself cannot determine the ideologies that go into the coverage of the news, and print news media have been no less conservative than electronic ones.

10. The conservative spin has been enriched by the many well-funded conservative foundations and think tanks that are eager to supply their facts and opinions to journalists and officials. See e.g., Trudy Lieberman, *Slanting the Story: The Forces that Shape the News* (New York: New Press, 2000).

11. Some of these groups would also become more affluent, but in actuality, liberal groups fundraise more successfully when conservatives are in power. Still, the funds they can obtain dwarf those that the conservative foundations regularly receive from corporate and other conservative donors.

12. As I suggested briefly in Chapter 2, the public journalism movement has tried to increase the frequency and intensity with which journalists consider citizens' issues, but the movement is still learning how to do so without interfering in the political process.

13. Some are even inherent in supplying national news per se and would be found in public television and radio if they had the funds to hire their own national and international newsgathering organizations.

14. The news organization is by no means unique. Many other organizations supplying professional goods or services are also organized as assembly lines, including parts of the academy.

15. Actually, news production also resembles assembly-line production, at least in print media, in that sections of the final product are put together separately in relatively independent groups before they are assembled into the final product. The groups responsible for putting together the individual sections of newspapers and news magazines, are usually divided into front and back of the book sections.

16. This account leaves out the subsequent manufacture and distribution of the final product, which is just about the only way in which blue-collar workers participate in news production.

17. In a sense investigative reporting is the luxury product of the news industry, which can earn it higher ratings and circulations, just as luxury products earn higher profits than standard ones in most other consumer industries.

18. As I use the terms here, events involve activities of one kind or another, in which people can be reported as doing something with other people, objects, or symbols. Statements involve spoken or written communications of one sort or another. Like all distinctions, this

one has fuzzy boundaries, but the terms involved are brief and to the point, so I will use them repeatedly.

19. By the same token, public officials can also release stories in the late afternoon on Fridays when they have the most chance of falling between journalistic schedules, and when audience interest is thought to be low. Such scheduling is regularly used for stories public officials would prefer not to release but that they cannot suppress.

20. The same process militates against oppositional sources making the news. They cannot supply news as quickly and easily, and lacking official authority, they must persuade editors and producers that their stories are newsworthy and accurate. All this takes time that reporters— and their superiors—do not often have.

21. Actually, the costs are shifted to the taxpayers.

22. This sentence is purposely written in the past tense, because if news about future wars are, like the Gulf War of the early 1990s, scripted by the Pentagon and if journalists can be prevented from doing their own reporting, war reporting might become another version of rewriting texts or voice-overs of official news handouts.

23. Howard S. Becker, et al., "Fieldwork with the Computer," *Qualitative Sociology* (Spring-Summer 1984): 16–33.

24. Actually, assignment editors carry out a prior data-reduction step; they decide which stories will actually be covered, thus also reducing the number of stories the editors and producers must squeeze into the newshole.

25. The internet's newsholes are in theory infinite, but websites that present the news are limited by the amount of advertising and other income that enables them to hire the journalists to fill the newshole, and to pay for active reporting. Without news organizations, the internet relies on leaks and even gossip that can be reported passively or almost so, but can nonetheless lead to scoops.

26. In electronic news media and also in news magazines, a secondary peg can be used to connect potentially usable stories to concurrently occurring events and statements. Scholars are sometimes surprised to find that routine papers delivered at an academic meeting appear in the news because the journalist can connect something in the paper to other news stories.

27. Time of occurrence and other peg criteria are not the sole determinants of newsworthiness, however, because editors and producers must still make decisions about a story's importance or interest, and often, must choose between two such stories that are likely to be fresh for about the same time.

28. For a helpful summary of this critique, see Pippa Norris, *A Virtuous Circle* (New York: Cambridge University Press, 2000), chapter 1.

29. See e.g., "The People, the Press and their Leaders," Los Angeles: The Center, 1995, 38.

30. Over the years, polling and other data have reported that most citizens do not begin to pay attention to the election campaign until after the party conventions or the World Series. The news media go into action much earlier—sometimes only weeks after the last election. Although media researchers support their news judgment by arguing that people learn what candidates stand for from detailed campaign reporting, it is not clear what they can learn if they are not or not yet paying attention to the election.

31. To be sure, campaign reforms and the proliferation of debates have persuaded journalists that they must also cover the "issues," but because candidates limit themselves to a small number and talk about them in generalities, especially when they cannot afford to alienate

any voters, the horse race remains the more interesting story. It is also the safer, politically neutral story, with candidates and others constantly searching for journalistic bias against them.

32. Of course, the debates also create another horse-race story, or more accurately, three horse races: instant analysts decide who won the debate, then who won the spinning of the debate, and once the polls have been completed who the respondents believe to have won the debate.

33. The majorities who are nonvoters in congressional elections rarely get even a single story.

34. The most important nonvoters are the people who vote normally but stay home in protest or for related reasons. They are also hard to cover, but ex post facto, their effect is often important and unmistakable.

35. An earlier discussion of the theory is in my "What Can Journalists Actually Do for Democracy?" *Press/Politics* 3, no. 4 (December 1998): 6–13.

36. Thomas Leonard, *The Power of the Press* (New York: Oxford University Press, 1986), chapter 7, quote on 193. See also James S. Ettema and Theodore L. Glasser, *Custodians of Conscience: Investigative Journalism and Public Virtue* (New York: Columbia University Press, 1998), chapter 3.

37. Michael Schudson, *The Good Citizen* (New York: Free Press, 1998).

38. For a somewhat different formulation, see Norris, *A Virtuous Circle*, chapter 2

39. Clean and competent government was a primary goal of the Progressive movement of the early twentieth century. Contemporary journalism still shares some of its values, but I wonder how many of today's journalists know about the origin of the movement and its values. The same question applies to the Progressives' political and class rationale: to empower the better-educated citizens in order to dismantle the urban political machines. The Progressives thought to reduce the influence of the less-educated, working-class, and presumably uninformed citizens whom the machine represented. See Schudson, *The Good Citizen*, 1998, 182–185. An interesting study could be done among contemporary journalists to see how many share these goals as they apply to today's political machines.

40. Actually, scholars are still debating what people actually learn from the news. Thus, one study concludes that they are poorly informed about important public officials and civic facts, while an earlier one indicates that they know enough about the relevant political facts and issues to make the most of the decisions required of them as citizens. See Michael X. Delli Carpini and Scott Keeter, *What Americans Know About Politics and Why It Matters* (New Haven: Yale University Press, 1996); and W. Russell Neuman, Marion R. Just, and Ann Crigler, *Common Knowledge: News and the Construction of Public Meaning* (Chicago: University of Chicago Press, 1992).

41. No one has yet figured out what needs of what publics are to be accommodated.

42. See e.g., Barry Glassner, *The Culture of Fear* (New York: Basic Books, 1999).

43. In fact, information levels are sometimes brought up when uninformed people disagree with the positions taken by experts, thus raising again the class conflicts that impelled Progressives to come up with the idea of the informed citizen in the first place.

44. Michael Schudson, "Why Conversation is not the Soul of Democracy," *Critical Studies in Mass Communications* no. 14 (December 1997): 297–309.

45. Meanwhile, the poll data suggest that people still talk politics mainly with their families.

46. For an analysis suggesting that discussion might enable journalists to "reclaim some of their lost authority in the public sphere," see Jay Rosen, "Politics, Vision and the Press: Toward

a Public Agenda for Journalists," in Twentieth Century Fund, *The New News versus the Old News* (New York: The Fund, 1992), 10.

47. A book of its own could be written about how the news media report the American family, social and community life, leisure behavior, various kinds of crime, and other everyday topics. The connections with democracy would be subtler, but such a book would raise the question of how the news media portray American society, how that portrait compares with those Americans draw for themselves, and how the various portraits affect government, politics, and democracy.

48. To be sure, the processes that occur between contribution and beneficial legislation do not take place in the presence of journalists but there are other ways of getting the necessary information.

49. Pollsters collect data on this general topic, and it sometimes appears in the news media when polls are reported in detail.

50. Unreasonably low but legal wages have been subjects of stories about Third World sweatshops, but only because antiglobalization movements and college students exposed pay scales and working conditions in these shops.

51. American poverty rates are based on a 1960s poverty definition that includes housing expenditures that have since increased dramatically. Unemployment rates ignore people who left the labor force because they could not find work, involuntary part-timers, temps who are hired as self-employed contractors, and the like.

52. A Nexis study of the reference to management and labor, conducted in seven major newspapers, two newsweeklies, and one network television news program for the years 1994-1996 showed that executives and managers received about 60 percent of the mentions, and workers and employees about 40 percent. Only the network news program deviated from the general pattern, workers and employees receiving 65 percent of the mentions, and executives and managers 35 percent.

I conducted the study while at the Media Studies Center, with Nexis data collected for me by Jocelyn Boryczka. The seven newspapers were divided between three national and four regional ones.

53. Jeff Madrick has found that the news media covered these subjects as signs of a "New Economy," but what was mostly new about that economy and thus newsworthy were the humongous increases in stock prices and the equally large paper profits of the executives of that economy. See Jeff Madrick, "The Business Media and the New Economy," Jean Shorenstein Center: Press, Politics, and Public Policy, research paper R-24, December 2001.

54. Actually, even when unions were stronger, they were newsworthy only when they struck, or when union corruption became visible.

55. In theory, local news media might be expected to cover such stories among major employers, but in practice, few do so.

56. My Media Studies Center research also showed that of four terms about employment and unemployment, downsizing received about 3 percent of the mentions. A 1995 study of NBC Nightly News showed that the program devoted 15 minutes that year to downsizing, as compared to 103 minutes on what it termed "government waste." Jonathan Cohn, "The Fleece Police," *The American Prospect* (May-June 1996), 12–13.

57. In all fairness to the journalists, the stock market displayed the same fear of inflation, and increases in unemployment were followed by increases in stock prices.

58. John Cassidy, "Gimme," *New Yorker*, 14 April 1997, 8–9. Although the journalists writing these stories sounded like representatives of "business interests," they were probably summarizing Federal Reserve Bank and other government press releases. Incidentally, four years later, obscenely high CEO incomes are being covered critically, especially the incomes of CEOs who have lost money for their employers.

   Many stories have been written, mostly in Style sections, about how the rich, and especially the newly rich spend their money, but only a rare few write the same story about median-income Americans.

59. The near total lack of research on the reporting of the Depression seems to me scandalous, but evidently journalism historians are driven by the same set of interests and blinders as their practitioner peers. For a notable exception, see James Boylan, "Publicity for the Great Depression," in Catherine D. Covert and John D. Stevens, eds., *Mass Media Between the Wars* (Syracuse: Syracuse University Press, 1984), chapter 10.

60. Such demands for censorship reappear every time the economy turns really sick.

61. Gary D. Best, *The Critical Press and the New Deal* (Westport, Conn.: Praeger, 1993), chapter 3. Perhaps newspaper business pages paid more attention to the problems associated with the Depression, but I could find no studies of them.

62. From this perspective, it appears that the news media are mostly devoted to news about a variety of industries supplying consumer goods and services, as well as sections of national and international news mostly devoted to government activities.

63. For a detailed study of business pages and their concentration on "personal finance," see Richard Parker, "The Revolution in America's Financial Industry: How Well is the Press Covering the Story?" Jean Shorenstein Center: Press, Politics, and Public Policy, (1999) 23–41.

64. According to media monitor David Rotbart, the number of business journalists rose from 4,200 in 1988 to over 12,000 in 1999. Diana M. Henriques, "Business Reporting: Behind the Curve," *Columbia Journalism Review* (November-December 2000): 18.

65. Michael Schudson, personal communication, 15 February 2000.

66. For this reason as for others, the concept of a political economy that connects polity and economy has never found favor in America, either among journalists or others. That the concept is at times identified as Marxist does not help either.

Chapter 4

1. Journalists may say that their job does not include creating effects, which is true insofar as they pay little explicit attention to the implications of the news they report. But insofar as they want the audience to be informed, public officials to be effective and honest, and the country to be democratic, they do want to have effects.

2. Most likely, a significant number of young people, particularly in the more conservative sectors of the country, waited to become sexually active until the mass media depictions legitimated such activity, but the role of the media in this process remains to be explored.

3. Among the researchers, most sociologists favor the limited effects theory, whereas researchers whose work involves research on pathology, such as psychologists, are more likely to endorse the hypodermic theory. Most cultural and literary theorists also endorse this theory, probably because they limit their research to the content of the media and then assume it must have powerful effects. Technological determinists favor the theory because they attribute strong effects to the technology regardless of what it communicates.

4. The story is told in Stephen Ansolabehere, Roy Behr, and Shanto Iyengar, *The Media Game: American Politics in the Television Age* (New York: Macmillan, 1993), 142. This case has been used to illustrate many other effects of television.

5. Selective perception came out of propaganda research done during World War II, but after being used in some election studies, dropped out of favor. This line of research, which seems extremely significant to me, has not been resumed, although parts of the concept have re-emerged in audience research inspired by "reception theory."

6. The reinforcement effect comes from Joseph T. Klapper, *The Effects of Mass Communication* (Glencoe, Ill.: Free Press, 1960).

7. I first undertook a review of the available news effects research, in a 1993, "Reopening the Black Box: Toward a Limited Effects Theory of the Mass Media," *Journal of Communication* 43 (Autumn 1993): 29–35. Subsequently, Dr. Patricia D'Andrade, my research assistant at the Media Studies Center, and I went through all the major books and journals in the field from 1990 to 1995, but found very few studies about the news. Most of these were correlational studies that provided no data for cause-effects conclusions. Consequently, I conducted only a partial review of the literature for 1995–2000.

8. In addition, my definition of effects is quite broad, so at times it also includes the consequences Merton described as manifest and latent functions.

9. Much of the laboratory research has been done by Shanto Iyengar and his associates. Their typical research method is "before-after," in which they interview the participants in the experiment to obtain their attitudes about the topic of study, show them actual or specially constructed news stories about the topic, then reinterview them for possible attitude change. Large numbers of the participants in the experiments change their minds to agree with the stories they have just seen. For an introduction to Iyengar's extensive research, see Shanto Iyengar and Donald R Kinder, *News That Matters* (Chicago: University of Chicago Press, 1987). Summaries of their studies may be found in Ansolabehere, Behr, and Iyengar, *The Media Game*.

10. Also, laboratory experimenters normally test the effects of one stimulus, such as a new bit of information at a time, but when people read or watch the news in their homes, they are exposed to many stimuli concurrently. As a result, laboratory findings cannot be extrapolated to normal news viewing and reading. For that and other reasons, my review of recent communication research did not include the findings of laboratory studies and the psychological and other journals that report such studies.

11. The few studies of how well the news audience comprehends the news, mostly about television news in Europe, suggest that many members comprehend only some of the stories they see, and are unable to understand unfamiliar technical, governmental, political, and other terms that journalists use in news reports.

12. A total news media blackout is probably impossible now, but they have occurred in the past, at least locally. For a study of one, see Bernard Berelson, "What Missing the Newspaper Means," in Paul Lazarsfeld and Frank Stanton, eds., *Communication Research, 1948–1949* (New York: Harper's, 1949), 111–129.

13. On 9/11, the journalists lost no time in reporting the president's slowness in returning to the White House, as well as the vice president's being sent off to an underground bunker.

14. In totalitarian countries, the regime would no longer have a medium to demonstrate its power and would be able to maintain that power only where it had armed soldiers.

15. For the same reason, public officials who know that many people pay less attention to the news on weekends sometimes release stories on Friday.

16. One would think the news media would have performed, or sponsored research on this topic by now, not only on how people use the various news media, but also which information sources they use to be informed when they eschew the news media.

17. I do not use the word "appears" accidentally, as pollsters sometimes hint at possible answers in the framing of their questions. In addition, the 40 percent or more of potential poll respondents who currently refuse to participate in surveys may include a number who cannot answer the questions. A study of what the people who do answer know about the subjects about which they are being quizzed would be useful.

18. Much of the news in underground newspapers in totalitarian societies is relevant to people's survival, which means that their readers' readiness to be informed is high, as is the journalists desire to inform them.

19. The public's need to know is a professional axiom that journalists use to explain and justify a large variety of news judgments. Academics sometimes use academic freedom very broadly to justify actions that have little or nothing to do with freedom.

20. Pew Center, "Times Mirror News Interest Index Study: Public Attentiveness to Major News Stories (1986–1999)," news release, 3 July 1999. I am indebted to Andrew Kohut and Kimberly Parker, Director and Research Director of the Pew Center respectively, for a great deal of data that, for reasons having nothing to do with them, did not make it into the book.

  The data are based on what people say they follow closely, and in some cases undoubtedly reflect publicly respectable answers. For example, news about celebrities were at the bottom of the list. More important, the closeness index favors breaking stories of brief duration, although it also reports the climaxes of long-running stories, such as the outcome of elections.

21. The inference is mine, and should not be blamed on the Pew Center. Between 1986 and 1999, of the total 700 stories that people said they followed closely, only 88 were followed "very closely" by 40 percent or more of the sample.

22. The actual question is: "Now I will read you a list of some stories covered by news organizations this past month. As I read each item, tell me if you happened to follow this news story very closely, fairly closely, not too closely, or not at all closely."

23. More than half of the top ten most closely followed news stories in the study were natural or human disasters.

24. Pew Center, "Terrorism Transforms News Interest," online report, 20 December 2001, Q.1b. By contrast, the top figure for the "U.S. Military Effort in Afghanistan" was 51 percent, reported in mid-October (Q.1a); that for the Enron bankruptcy and its impact on the retirement investments of Enron employees was 11 percent (Q.1e).

25. These informal news reporters may be similar to those who media researchers once called "opinion leaders." See Elihu Katz and Paul F. Lazarsfeld, *Personal Influence* (Glencoe, Ill.: Free Press, 1955). I would not be surprised if such opinion leaders still exist, not only as informal journalists but as informal commentators, with information and opinions on subjects ranging from the national news to the latest department store sales.

26. Audience researchers in the print news media count not only the people who buy or subscribe to a newspaper or news magazine, but also the estimated "pass-alongs" who constitute another informal audience.

27. The importance of this news source was emphasized when the Gore presidential campaign staff sought to reconstruct the Gore public persona after seeing a parody about it on "Saturday Night Live." The comics' version of the news may create oppositional effects, or more likely, feed oppositional predispositions. No doubt print media political cartoons have long played the same role.

28. On legitimation, see also Gladys E. Lang and Kurt Lang, *The Battle for Public Opinion: The President, the Press and the Polls During Watergate* (New York: Columbia University Press, 1983), chapter 7. The same process that makes legitimation possible also produces the comics and others who act to delegitimate the same phenomena.

29. For some people, especially those seeing the news media as representing and publicizing ruling elites, the news may be delegitimating.

30. Journalists thereby reduce what social scientists call pluralistic ignorance—when people are not aware that others share the knowledge that they believe these others are ignorant about.

31. Journalists may feel like flag waving themselves, because they are often caught between their roles as citizens and those as neutral or detached journalists.

32. For an incisive analysis of the exclusion of minor party candidates, and their resulting inability to try to replace the major party ones, see Joshua Meyrowitz, "Visible and Invisible Candidates," *Political Communication* 11 (1994): 145–64. As Left media critics point out repeatedly, the news media can use the exclusion of minority viewpoints as a method of political censorship.

33. Many advertisers are allowed to withdraw advertising when a news story contradicts their message. Thus, airline ads become scarce when the news media report a plane crash.

34. This flies in the belief that journalists set the agenda for the news audience: they tell people what to think about, but not what to think. Actually, much of the time, the journalists are the agenda setters, but like college professors, journalists do not like to admit when their audience sets the agenda. The notion of agenda-setting comes from Maxwell E. McCombs and D. L. Shaw, "The Agenda Setting Function of Mass Media," *Public Opinion Quarterly* 36 (1972): 176–187.

35. This process is strengthened by the fact that notable events also generate polls and poll questions.

36. On such stories as on other foreign news, the news media often stay close to the government's foreign policy.

37. The best-known recent claim of news media effects is Robert Putnam's argument, mentioned earlier, that watching television is a major factor in the decline of political participation. Putnam supplies a good deal of data, mostly correlational, for his hypothesis, but Pippa Norris points out that education and age are more important factors in political behavior than television viewing. See Robert Putnam, "Tuning In, Tuning Out: The Strange Disappearance of Social Capital in America," *PS: Political Science and Politics* 27 (December 1995): 664–683; and Pippa Norris, "Does Television Erode Social Capital? A Reply to Putnam," *PS: Political Science and Politics* 28 (September 1996): 474–480.

38. About 20 years ago, David Phillips suggested that the news media reporting of prominent suicides was linked to an increase in suicides by the general public, and that the news media had an imitation effect. But later analyses have questioned Phillips's analysis. See e.g., Kenneth A. Bollen and David P. Phillips, "Imitative Suicides: A National Study of the Effects of Television News Stories," *American Sociological Review* 47 (December 1982):

802–809; and Kenneth A. Bollen and David D. Phillips, "Imitation and Suicide: A Reexamination of the Werther Effect," *American Sociological Review* 49 (June 1984): 427–436. Imitations are probably inspired more often by entertainment media that are more likely to supply relevant operational detail about an illegal act than the news media.

39. A.M. Rosenthal, *Thirty Eight Witnesses: The Kitty Genovese Story* (New York: McGraw Hill, 1964). The local instances usually cease after a few weeks when editors or producers have decided that the story is no longer newsworthy.

40. The profession awards many such prizes. Even if it does not win a prize, an exposé with visible effects, such as the successful prosecution of the villains, is viewed as a highpoint of a journalistic career.

41. Media researchers describe this process as "refracting" or "framing" the story. On refraction, see Gladys E. Lang and Kurt Lang, *The Battle for Public Opinion* (New York: Columbia University Press, 1983); on framing, see Gaye Tuchman, *Making News* (New York: Free Press 1978); and Todd Gitlin, *The Whole World is Watching* (Berkeley: University of California Press, 1980).

42. The highlighting was not unusual; by journalists' criteria of newsworthiness, that was the most important part of the story. How much the success of the legislation was due to the television film is hard to measure.

Highlighting the antiwar marches of the 1960s and the globalization marches of the 1990s through the police rioting and other violence these generated had a very different effect; they diverted attention from the positions being advocated by the marchers.

43. Actually, most investigative reporting seems to begin with a leak from a victim or observer of illegal or corrupt behavior.

44. The classic text is Lincoln Steffens, *The Autobiography of Lincoln Steffens* (New York: Harcourt Brace, 1931).

45. The reverse effect, made possible by the conservative Republican takeover of many of the country's courts, is retaliation with libel and other suits that have restricted the freedom of journalists to undertake such exposés.

46. Michael Schudson, *The Power of the News* (Cambridge: Harvard University Press, 1995); also his *The Sociology of the News* (New York: Norton, 2002).

47. TV cameras are more effective in this respect than the print reporter's notebook.

48. Ronald Reagan was allowed to make mistakes, perhaps because they did not conflict with his image as the "Great Communicator."

49. Clinton's luck ended when he pardoned major lawbreakers just before leaving the White House. The misdeed may be forgotten again, but sometimes the deviant behavior tarnishes long-range or historical reputations, as it has for Richard Nixon.

50. Not coincidentally, however, some media critics argue that the kind of watchdog news in which "60 Minutes" specializes make it more of a cops-and-robbers show than a news program.

51. In addition, the *Times* probably undertakes more investigative reporting, local and national, per inch of newshole or by any other per capita measure, than all other American news media.

52. During the recession that began in 2001, layoffs have been reported far more systematically, although the term "downsizing" was not revived.

53. The Pentagon's self-protective policy resulted from its inaccurate conclusion that the journalists' considerable freedom of access during the Vietnam War was a major factor in that war's inglorious conclusion.

54. Actually, the Pentagon was not entirely successful, because some journalists were able to report what appears to have been the promiscuous killing of fleeing Iraqi soldiers after the end of the war.

   The Pentagon was also protected to some extent by the journalists themselves, since they have never been able or willing to report the military's illegal activities, or the incompetence of its officers. More often than not, they have left that chapter of the first draft of history to the historians.

55. For an analysis that sees the news media exerting stronger political effects, see Timothy B. Cook, *Governing with the News* (Chicago: University of Chicago Press, 1998).

56. This paragraph and the previous one is indebted to Michael Schudson, who has a better eye for the routine functions and effects of the news media than any other researcher.

57. Elie Abel, *Leaking: Who Does it? Who Benefits? At What Costs?* (New York: Priority Press, 1987).

58. They also use other inputs, including suggestions and reactions from constituents. Some elected officials treat the way news stories are framed as intentional or unintentional editorial comment that is raw material for the climate.

59. The news media's political effects are distorted by the fact that their coverage of politics has itself become a subject of the news. The effects of journalists reporting on themselves should make an interesting study in the future.

60. Michael Schudson's historical analysis of political communication in the United States should act as a corrective to any temptation to ascribe unusual causal power to the news media. See Schudson, *The Good Citizen*.

61. Although media researchers have been preoccupied with studying the role of the media in elections sui generis, and at great expense, for over a generation, every election is different. Comparing the roles and effects of the news media in different types of elections would be useful, but the search for general effects common to all elections overestimates the political effects of the news media and depoliticizes the elections themselves.

62. As far as I can tell, no one has ever tried to measure the effect of all the handshaking, or whether voters believe that a candidate shows his or her willingness to do something about a problem by shaking hands near a relevant institution.

63. Television may also have spurred the selection of telegenic candidates, although the ability to obtain campaign funds trumps physical attractiveness. So far there is no evidence that telegenic candidates win more elections or research about how voters decide which candidate is more telegenic. Even the candidates' ability to perform on television and still be presidential is only one criterion of electability among many, as the 2000 election demonstrated anew.

64. In addition, debate moderators are screened by the candidates' staffs and the journalists who survive the screening process are unlikely to be aggressive or to have made what could be perceived as critical comments about the campaigners.

65. Actually, the relatively small sums paid by most campaign contributors can result in multimillion dollar paybacks by grateful politicians. In effect, elected representatives come cheap, and sell government even more cheaply. In addition, both parties stratify contributors by size of contribution, with the highest contributors receiving the largest rewards, which in turn presumably raises the size of the contributions.

66. Whether the endless repetition adds viewer hostility or boredom to visibility deserves to be studied.

67. Foreign governments have always scoured the routine news of other countries for information that could be reframed by their intelligence agencies for use in espionage and the like.

68. The effect is sometimes called the "CNN effect," because CNN was the first worldwide news organization that also provided round-the-clock news programs. For an interesting discussion of the effect and its policy consequences when it first began to operate, see Lloyd N. Cutler, "Foreign Policy on Deadline," *Foreign Policy* (Fall 1984): 113–128.

69. Conservative ideologues have been particularly active in blaming journalists for their reporting because as citizens many vote Democratic. However, these conservatives are almost alone in failing to notice that the Democrats have not been liberal for quite a while. For the canonical social scientists' litany on this subject, see S. Robert Lichter, Stanley Rothman, and Linda Lichter, *The Media Elite* (Bethesda, Md.: Adler and Adler, 1986).

70. Although the Right and Left try to use all the mass media to further their objectives, they also blame "the media" for some of their ideological and other failures.

71. In some quarters, "the media" is also a code word for "the Jews," who are believed not only to own all of the mass media but to control the country through them.

72. Perhaps they will only become apparent retroactively through future historical research.

73. Unfortunately, no one studied attention spans before television and few researchers have done so since.

74. See, e.g., Joshua Meyrowitz, *No Sense of Place* (New York: Oxford University Press, 1985), and Jeffrey L. Scheuer, *The Soundbite Society:* Television and the American Mind (New York: Four Walls and Eight-Windows, 1999).

75. There is also the methodological problem of how one compares today's America with the country as it existed before the coming of the news media and especially the mass news media, and how one could isolate changes that can be attributed to the news media.

76. Dwight MacDonald, "Our Invisible Poor," The *New Yorker*, January 19, 1969, 82–132.

77. It would also be undesirable, because if the news could have such political effects, some journalists might be tempted to take power themselves.

Chapter 5

1. For an earlier version of some of these ideas, see my "What Can Journalists Actually Do for American Democracy?" *Press and Politics* 3 (Winter 1998): 6–12.

2. To be sure, most people, including professionals, do a lot of informal talking with peers, but journalists seem to try to minimize their contact with nonpeers.

3. See also Pew Center for Civic Journalism, "Journalism Interactive," news release, 26 July 2001.

4. If students are assigned to different neighborhoods they can come together at the end of the course and brief each other about audience diversity.

5. Ideally, journalists should learn how more of their news audience might be transformed into news buffs. I don't know whether this is possible, and who could bring about the transformation.

6. The Pentagon works hard to develop local stories about what military personnel from local areas are doing in peacetime as in wartime efforts. However, few American or foreign newsmakers have the Pentagon's public-relations budget.

7. Objectivity is epistemologically impossible, because the moment journalists ask questions they select from a large number of possible ones. The fact that journalists have traditionally

seen participation through the eyes of public officials does not make that practice objective. Adding the perspective of the citizenry cannot be objective either. Both kinds of coverage can be detached, however, as long as journalists answer the questions empirically rather than with their opinions.

8. On slow news days, stories can be written about why there was no trouble.

9. Individual personal requests should be excluded, but large numbers of people making similar personal requests becomes a politically relevant story.

10. Particularly thoughtful communications, or those with an uncommon viewpoint might also be newsworthy, and perhaps even a "letters to the politicians" feature might be helpful.

11. James Lemert, "News Context and the Elimination of Mobilizing Information," *Journalism Quarterly* (Summer 1984): 243–249. Rod Spaw has described information useful for participating citizens as "community journalism." (Personal communication, 5 March 2001.)

12. Television equivalents can be found on local television news programs.

13. The resemblance of this version of the action line to "60 Minutes" should be obvious.

14. I pointed out in Chapter 2 that public journalism, also called civic journalism, was founded in the early 1990s by journalist Davis Merritt and journalism professor Jay Rosen as a community-centered form of journalism to correct what they saw as the excessively detached and positivist coverage of mainstream journalism. See Davis B. Merritt, *Public Journalism and Public Life* (Hillside, N.J.: Erlbaum, 1995), and Jay Rosen, *Getting the Connections Right; Public Journalism and the Troubles in the Press* (New York: Twentieth-Century Fund, 1996).

15. For a useful review of public journalism projects see Charlotte Grimes, "Whither the Civic Journalism Bandwagon," Jean Shorenstein Center: Press, Politics, and Public Policy, discussion paper D-36, February 1991. A thoughtful critique of public journalism is Michael Schudson, "The Public Journalism Movement and Its Problems," in Doris Graber, Denis McQuail, and Pippa Norris, eds., *Politics of News; News of Politics* (Washington, D.C.: CQ Press, 1998), 132–147.

16. "Civic Catalyst," the newsletter published by the Pew Center for Civic Journalism, reports on a range of public journalism projects in its quarterly issues.

17. They have also been bitterly criticized by widely respected high-level and other journalists for going beyond reporting to becoming quasi-participants in the political process. The criticism is justified if journalists give up their neutrality and come too close to acting as public officials. However, the critics of public journalism sometimes do not see how much their seemingly neutral selection of sources and the reporting that follows can ultimately supply publicity for public officials.

18. Analytic or interpretive news allows the reporter who has covered the story, or any other journalist informed about it, to add observations about the meaning of, or to speculate about the whys of, events and statements that have been described—or to do almost anything else that adds to the story, including a touch of personal opinion.

19. Such information may also be useful for the people and groups that oppose altering the status quo.

20. When citizens can analyze and explain problems, public officials may also be discouraged from proposing symbolic and other solutions that do little to solve the problem. Conversely, the analyses and explanations may also persuade people that they lack the power or the ability to bring about change.

21. Melani McAlister, "Television, Terrorism and the Making of Incomprehension," *Chronicle of Higher Education,* 7 December 2001, B13–14.

22. Along this line, William Kovach and Tom Rosenstiel suggest that "journalism is by nature reactive and practical, rather than philosophical and introspective." *Elements of Journalism,* 41. For their critical take on "interpretive journalism," see ibid., 55.

23. Given shortages of airtime and print space, journalists tend to end up with reasons and motives, notably the latter because they are almost always more dramatic. Their favorite guesses about reasons and causes include, aside from villains, far-seeing politicians, or less-far-seeing ones who are yearning for higher office. Journalistic explainers also turn to big events, like a war or a change in governments, or broad cultural trends like sexual revolutions and permissiveness. In addition, journalists treat generations as social bodies that act similarly and collectively, and can therefore be used to explain events and trends of all kinds. Decades, or rather, selected major events that are used to characterize decades, can also be used to explain elements in American life. Journalists can apparently not get along without such stereotypical causal notions as "baby boomers" and "the sixties."

24. The internet is technically flexible enough to overcome problems of presentation but today's internet websites lack reasons and funds for hiring the news organizations necessary to execute explanatory journalism. Thus, it is too early to ask how many people will read complicated stories on the web.

25. Also, too often a state of war exists between the two professions, for in the social sciences, journalistic is frequently a synonym for superficiality, while journalists condemn the social scientists' predilection for abstract theory and incomprehensible jargon. Although both professions would benefit from a more cooperative relationship, neither now has an incentive to make peace. One solution may lie with the public intellectual, who can translate social science information to inform journalists, or the general public directly.

26. Dramatic topics like the contested 2000 presidential election or 9/11 and the rise of terrorism are frequently turned into quickly produced books that deliver at least some explanations.

27. Human action is always based on a mixture of values, facts, and opinions, and perhaps an increase in the use of informed opinion would help some people in the news audience think about current events.

28. Columnists are particularly vulnerable to this shortcoming. Over the years they develop constituencies who share their values and subtly encourage them to develop an ideological or political line. No wonder pundit is becoming a pejorative term.

29. Indeed, many other reporters could benefit from such training, particularly those who begin their legwork with a conclusion derived from their own values and then look for sources and information to support that conclusion. Unlike ideologues, they usually do so unintentionally, so they should benefit from a little training in how to think journalistically.

30. The success of op-ed pages and cable television talk shows suggests the possibility that opinion news might also help increase the news audience.

31. More columnists would also be desirable if they spanned more of the ideological spectrum. News media catering to educated audiences could make a place for "public intellectuals," i.e., academics and other intellectuals who can write in clear and jargon-free English.

32. For an argument against the existence of the public sphere, see Michael Schudson, *The Power of News* (Cambridge: Harvard University Press, 1995), chapter 9. Today's Conception of the

public sphere is by Juergen Habermas. For a short summary of his conception, see Juergen Habermas, "The Public Sphere," in Chandra Mukerji and Michael Schudson, eds., *Rethinking Popular Culture* (Berkeley: University of California Press, 1991), chapter 14.

33. Herbert J. Gans, *Deciding What's News* (New York: Pantheon, 1979), chapter 10.

34. Because of increasingly easier access to foreign news on the internet, in large cities, and on cable television, people can now construct their own multiple perspectives. Unfortunately, foreign journalists pay little attention to American domestic news, however.

35. The British "press lord," Lord Northcliffe, once underlined the diversity of the news by defining it as "information that someone, somewhere, wants to suppress." "Everything else," adds Reuven Frank, "is advertising." (Reuven Frank, personal communication.)

Louis Wirth's sociological version of a similar point argued that "society rests upon a divergent interpretation of the 'factual' situation . . . since every assertion of a 'fact' about the social world touches the interest of some individual or group." Louis Wirth, preface by Karl Mannheim in *Ideology and Utopia* (New York: Harcourt Brace, 1936), xvii.

36. Robert M. Entman and Andrew Rojecki, *The Black Image in the White Mind: Media and Race in America* (Chicago: University of Chicago Press, 2000).

37. The articles and other materials on the series can be found in *New York Times, How Race is Lived in America* (New York: Times Books, 2001).

38. The upper-middle class may be culturally and politically dominant, but when pollsters give respondents a choice between describing themselves as working class or middle class, about the same proportions put themselves in each group.

39. In both places, class trumps race, because discrimination against racial minorities who can think and write in a middle-class style is disappearing fast. However, currently neither news organizations nor the academy can effectively compete with corporations and law firms for upper-middle-class blacks, Hispanics, and Asians.

40. Not so long ago, television correspondents with southern or midwest accents could still be heard on network television.

41. For that matter, journalists from unfree presses could add another perspective, including on the practices of America's kind of free press.

42. Trained but unpaid volunteers would be ideal. Some journals of opinion survive because their staff includes such volunteers, but these write commentaries and reviews, and rarely undertake time-consuming legwork.

43. This format has long been used by the PBS Evening News Hour.

44. A number of op-ed pages are already nationally syndicated, as are the comics. Apparently local papers do not compete by each having its own unique comic strips.

45. The *Washington Post National Weekly Edition* accompanies some of its columnists with cartoons, often with very different opinions. The juxtaposition demonstrates graphically that alternative viewpoints exist, but sometimes additional reactions to both would enrich them both.

46. Print media should also be able to reprint some of television's late-night satire—as some newspapers already do—and television news could benefit from showing some relevant newspaper cartoons.

47. Fiction is used here in its traditional popular meaning, not as a postmodern substitute for concepts for understanding and accounts of the empirical world. For a constructive and thoughtful discussion of blurring the distinctions betwen news and entertainment, see

Bruce A. Williams and Michael X. Delli Carpini, "Heeeeeeeeeeeeere's Democracy!" *Chronicle of Higher Education*, 19 April 2002, B14–15.

48. I purposely omit political films with fairly overt messages, such as the anti-Nixon satire "Dick," or pro-union films such as "Norma Rae."

49. The film "All the President's Men," the retelling of the Watergate saga, could be described as a film docudrama.

50. Even now, internet news websites could offer links to relevant fiction.

51. News fiction makes deliberate political statements about the world, but so do other kinds of fiction. In fact, virtually all forms of art and entertainment have political subtexts, deliberate or otherwise, and many could be used to enhance or elaborate on the news.

52. Nonfiction news also sometimes oversimplifies for storytelling purposes, however.

53. Beats usually come into two kinds. One is political, and the larger news media at least have beats for each branch of the federal government, foreign countries, as well as some major American cities. The other kind of beat is professional, which includes, among others, medicine, law, health, science, and the arts, high and low.

 Both kinds of beats have inherent problems. The political beats require rapport and trust with sources, but too much and too long-standing a rapport can lead to friendships with sources, resulting in self-censorship and unconscious biases.

 Professional beats suffer from the fact that too many experts do not understand that journalists must report to a lay audience. As a result, experts accuse journalists of oversimplification, while journalists accuse experts of being unwilling to share their expertise with lay people.

54. The news media also rely on professional experts, such as doctors, lawyers, and in time of war, retired generals. They look for experts who can avoid using professional jargon, and cable television news could not survive without them.

55. For a thoughtful statement of the practitioner position, though not of the simple traditional kind, see Betty Medsger, "Winds of Change: Challenges Confronting Journalism Education," (New York: Freedom Forum, 1996).

56. Journalism schools appear to be experiencing some of the same pressures felt by all professional schools: to be more conventionally academic and academically respectable; and to conduct "scholarly" research, particularly in mass communication.

 Conducting academic mass-communications research would be useful if its research were designed to be helpful to journalists, but as a PhD program, mass communications has no incentive to move in this direction. At the same time, like most of the research disciplines bred in professional schools, mass communications has many of the vices and too few of the virtues of academic research. It is thus no accident that much of the best media research has been the work of social scientists, beginning with Paul Lazarsfeld.

57. They should also obtain some new methodological skills, beginning with introductory statistics, which too many reporters still cannot handle. As a result, they are unable to interpret properly the ever-more-important news polls, economic analyses, and newsworthy research reports.

58. Any program that teaches both journalists and fledgling scholars would be a blessing for both. Journalists might learn some of the analytic skills and the theoretical perspectives of scholars. The scholars, on the other hand, may become interested in the "real world" topics that journalists write about and drop some of the intellectually more dubious pursuits,

as well as the jargon, constructed in the ivory tower. In time, the destructive miscommunication and the considerable hostility that now exist between the journalistic and scholarly communities might shrink and then disappear.

59. See also Gilbert Cranberg, Randall Bezanson, and John Soloski, *Taking Stock: Journalism and the Publicly Traded Newspaper Company* (Ames: Iowa State University Press, 2001).

60. Often prestige is sought as a substitute for or an avenue to power, but the big firms have other ways of obtaining power.

61. For one hopeful charting, see Max Frankel, "The Nirvana News," *New York Times Magazine*, 9 July 2000, 16, 18.

Chapter 6

1. The six are not meant to be comprehensive or even to take account of the many others that have been made over the years. For other recent proposals toward greater democracy, see e.g., Benjamin R. Barber, *Strong Democracy* (Berkeley: University of California Press, 1984), 267–311; Lawrence R. Jacobs and Robert Y. Shapiro, *Politicians Don't Pander* (Chicago: University of Chicago Press, 2000), chapters 9, 10; and Derek Bok, *The Trouble with Government* (Cambridge: Harvard University Press, 2001). See also Michael B. Katz, *The Price of Citizenship* (New York: Metropolitan Books, 2001); and Alex Keyssar, *The Right to Vote: The Contested History of Democracy in the United States* (New York: Basic Books, 2000). An earlier version of some of my proposals are in my *Middle American Individualism* (New York: Free Press, 1988), chapter 6.

2. See e.g., Frances F. Piven and Richard A. Cloward, *Why Americans Still Don't Vote* (Boston: Beacon, 2000).

3. In addition, the Supreme Court would have to reverse its earlier decision that a campaign contribution is equivalent to free speech.

4. The conventional argument for long campaigns is their ability to educate the voters about the candidates, but a number of voters have made up their minds even before the primaries have ended and each party's candidate is known. Most of the undecideds do not tune into the campaigning until the time symbolized by the end of baseball's World Series.

5. Possibly, a reduction in overall campaign advertising might lead to a greater reliance on negative advertising, but it seems to be politically dangerous sufficiently often enough to discourage greater reliance on it.

6. They could even turn to direct bribery, which remains popular all over the world.

7. The unions and a few other groups supposedly represent some of the less affluent citizens, and the least affluent are spoken for by a handful of organizations or can resort to peaceful or violent protest. But none of these means appear to be politically very effective.

8. Some of the shorter and less costly polls may obtain response rates as low as 15 percent. (Personal communication, Robert Y. Shapiro, 6 November 2000.) On the democratic potentials of polling, see George Gallup and Samuel F. Ray, *Pulse of Democracy* (New York: Simon & Schuster, 1940); Jacobs and Shapiro, *Politicians Don't Pander*, especially chapter 10, and Justin Lewis, *Constructing Public Opinion* (New York: Columbia University Press, 2001).

9. In all fairness, pollsters also ask questions they believe to be of interest to the citizenry.

10. Some similar and other proposals regarding polling can be found in Jacobs and Shapiro, *Politicians Don't Pander*. See also Lewis, *Constructing Public Opinion*.

11. Focus group responses are too easily influenced by the makeup of the group and by its articulate members. They also do not lend themselves easily to probing questions.

12. This assumes, however, and perhaps unrealistically, that the generically undercounted population that is not found by the census and does not get on any voting lists is picked up in the pollsters' national samples.

13. Herbert J. Gans, "Time for an Employees Lobby," *Social Policy* 24 (Winter 1993): 35–38. One such lobby, Working Today, represents contingent and other independent or contract workers. Some economic research organizations and others also do occasional economic lobbying.

14. There is also no reason that a particular interest cannot be pressed by both member and nonmember lobbies.

15. "Mediating structures" were developed in a pamphlet by Peter Berger and John Neuhaus "To Empower People" (Washington, D.C.: American Enterprise Institute for Public Policy Research, 1977), who had in mind local nonprofit institutions and associations, including churches. The points of light came from the elder George Bush, and his son later proposed "faith-based" organizations.

16. Many of them also stopped being civil, and helped to revive the party struggles that were going on during the pre-Communist era.

17. Lobbies can probably not participate in disruption, however, except at the cost of precluding any future political usefulness.

18. This, however, is true of all large and democratically run organizations that are not pursuing a single purpose or interest.

19. Watchdog reporting should publicize the lobbies that take euphemistic names to hide their actual purposes and funding sources, their occasional conduct of fake polls and letter writing campaigns, and other unethical if not necessarily illegal practices.

20. Actually, White House staffs are currently covered as little as lobbies; so are the staffs who do much of the work of the legislative, executive, and judicial branches, and as people inside the Beltway know, sometimes make policy for the country.

21. They should really be citizens of the political economy, if that existed as a visible and functioning body.

22. The list is deceptive, because economic and political battles will be fought over what powers and how much power should go to management, labor, customers, shareholders, and the general public.

23. I assume that the country is too large to be governed by the trio of capital, labor, and government that has successfully governed some of the Western European welfare states.

24. For a review of recent citizenship theorizing, see Will Kymlicka and Wayne Norman, "Return of the Citizen: A Survey of Recent Work on Citizenship Theory," in Ronald Beiner, ed., *Theorizing Citizenship* (Albany, N.Y.: State University of New York Press, 1995), 283–322.

INDEX OF SUBJECTS

INDEX OF NAMES